Lecture Notes in Economics and Mathematical Systems

Managing Editors: M. Beckmann and W. Krelle

316

R. L. Basmann D. J. Slottje
K. Hayes J. D. Johnson
D. J. Molina

The Generalized Fechner-Thurstone Direct Utility Function and Some of its Uses

Springer-Verlag

New York Berlin Heidelberg London Paris Tokyo

Authors

R. L. Basmann
Department of Economics
SUNY Binghamton
Binghamton, NY 13901, USA

D. J. Slottje
Department of Economics
Southern Methodist University
Dallas, TX 75275, USA

K. Hayes
Department of Economics
Southern Methodist University
Dallas, TX 75275, USA

J. D. Johnson
Department of Economics
University of Mississippi
University, MS 38677, USA

D. J. Molina
Department of Economics
University of North Texas
Denton, TX 76201, USA

ISBN 0-387-96853-9 Springer-Verlag New York Berlin Heidelberg
ISBN 3-540-96853-9 Springer-Verlag Berlin Heidelberg New York

Printing and binding: Druckhaus Beltz, Hemsbach/Bergstr.
2847/3140-543210

To:

J. Nicholas Slottje

David Francis Slottje Jr.

Spencer Slottje

Kimberly Kanani Hayes

Lauren Makena Johnson

with love.

Preface

This book stems from research that Basmann, Molina and Slottje began together in 1980. Basmann had explored many of the concepts we will discuss below twenty five years earlier, but had put the work aside to concentrate on econometric statistics and didn't return to the subject of this book until 1980. The subject matter of this monograph has elicited some controversy and as we hope to show as the reader progresses, most of it is unnecessary. The material in Chapter Two follows closely from a paper we published in the *Journal of Institutional and Theoretical Economics* and we are grateful to the publisher for permission to use the material again. The second chapter also includes several new sections which have never been published before. The same is true of Chapter Five where we thank the American Statistical Association for permission to reprint some of our earlier results and again we have added sections never published. Chapter Six is based on a forthcoming article in *Economica* and the subsequent chapters will all be submitted to journals at the time this monograph goes to press, which is one of the aims of Springer-Verlag's series in mathematical economics.

Many individuals have provided helpful comments on this research over the past few years without being implicated for any errors in anyway. They include; Bill Barnett, Ray Battalio, Mike Baye, Dan Black, Frank Cowell, Charles Diamond, Erwin Diewert, Chris Fawson, James Foster, Frank Gollop, Terence Gorman, Joe Hadar, Joe Hirschberg, Arthur Lewbel, Dale Jorgenson, Essie Maasoumi, Mike Nieswiadomy, Dan Slesnick, Tom Stoker and Hans Theil. Finally, we wish to thank Sherry Jackson, Janet Thoele and Pontip Vattakavanich for much patience and expert typing.

Contents

Chapter 1

Introduction

Whenever a neoclassical direct utility function is in close (even perfect) agreement with consumer behavior data, there is always an alternative direct utility function that agrees at least as closely with the same data. By 'agreement' we mean that a real sample S of consumer data assigns significant *likelihood ratio* support to the parameters of utility function in question when the latter is tested as a null hypothesis nested within a broader class of utility functions.[1] Existence of this equally well (if not better) fitting alternative to such a neoclassical direct utility function has considerable significance for the rational conduct of potential problem analysis in the policy-making arena. [We shall give important examples later in this book.]

However the *nonuniqueness* of any neoclassical utility function on empirical data is rarely mentioned in the literature of economic theory. The inherent impossibility of any neoclassical utility functions to acquire the greater observational support in a fair likelihood ratio test against *non-neoclassical* alternatives appears to be little understood among economists generally. There is some recognition that a successful "fit" of the CES form cannot possibly warrant the conclusion that tastes remained constant in a time-series, *cf.* Landsburg, 1981, p. 103. Generality of *nonuniqueness* was too cryptically demonstrated in Basmann et al., 1983, p.412.

---

[1]Strict neoclassical direct utility functions (Basmann et al., 1985b, pp. 75-76) that are popular among microtheorists have fared very badly as null hypotheses, however. This is especially the case with the CES (constant elasticity of substitution form) used by Landsburg, 1981 and its limiting forms, "Cobb-Douglas" and Leontief.

This introduction presents a short proof and explanation of this *nonunique-ness* of empirically realistic neoclassical direct utility functions.

Let S be a batch of observed vectors of price, total expenditure, and quantities consumed by a group of one of more individual consumers.[2]

Let $V(X;\psi)$ be a direct utility function[3] that is strictly neoclassical.[4]

Theorem 1 (Nonuniqueness) *If a strictly neoclassical direct utility function $V(\mathbf{X};\psi)$ rationalizes the data batch S, then $V(X;\psi)$ cannot be unique.*

Proof of Theorem 1 *follows directly from the following theorem:*

Theorem 2 (Existence of a Direct Utility Function) *If X, p, and M satisfy the linear budget constraint (1.1), then there is a direct utility function, $U(X;\theta)$, having the form illustrated below that is maximized by the consumer group's choice of X.*

The direct utility function may be unique for some data batches S. However notice that the second theorem implies the nonuniqueness of every other direct utility function $W(X;\psi)$ whether or not the taste-descriptive parameter ψ is strictly independent of budget constraint prices and total expenditure.

Now let S be an arbitrarily large sample of observed vectors (X, p, M) from an exactly repeatable, absolutely flawless *revealed preference* experiment. The subject of the experiment is an individual consumer, p is an n-vector of positive prices and M is the total expenditure the consumer is allowed to make during any specified session of the experiment. Vector (p, M) is under experimental control and is changed from session to session. X is the consumer response; it is an n-vector of nonnegative

---

[2]X is an n-vector of nonnegative quantities. p is an n-vector of positive prices. M is total expenditure on X at prices p.

[3]For the present discussion assume that all utility functions denoted in this article possess continuous second-order derivatives with respect to components of X. This assumption causes no loss of generality that is essential. A general analysis would add nothing to the main point of this article *cf* Samuelson and Sato 1984, p. 589.

[4]I.e., the taste-descriptive parameter-vector ψ is strictly independent of changes in total expenditure M and budget constraint price vector p. In case ψ is differentiable with respect to p and M, strict neoclassical assumptions imply that all partial derivatives are exactly zero for every (p, M).

quantities chosen by the consumer subject to the budget constraint determined by (p, M). Let us assume that the consumer allocates all of M to the expenditure on commodities $i = 1, \ldots, n$, *viz*,

$$\sum_{i=1}^{n} p_i X_i = M \tag{1.1}$$

for all observations (X, p, M) that come in question. A necessary consequence is that the consumer's response (demand) results in maximization of a direct utility function that has the *Generalized Fechner-Thurstone* (GFT) form.

Seo (1973) demonstrated[5] that Arrow's (1961) claim that *any* system of demand functions satisfying the linear budget constraint above can always be written as:

$$x_i = M \left[\frac{g_i (p_1, \ldots, p_n, M)}{p_i \sum_{k=1}^{n} g_k (p_1, \ldots, p_n, M)} \right], \quad i = 1, 2, \ldots, n. \tag{1.2}$$

needed to be extended to:

$$x_i = \frac{g_i (p_1, \ldots, p_n, M)}{p_i \sum_{j=1}^{n} g_j (p_1, \ldots, p_n, M)} \left[M - \sum_{k=1}^{n} \gamma_k p_k \right] + \gamma_i, \tag{1.3}$$
$$i = 1, 2, \ldots, n.$$

where:

$$g_i (p_1, \ldots, p_n, M) > 0 \quad \forall i, \quad \left[M - \sum_{k=1}^{n} \gamma_k p_k \right] > 0.$$

so as to include the case where the γ_i's are not equal to zero.

Since any system of demand functions can be expressed in the form of (1.3) above finding a utility function that yields (1.3), when maximized subject to a linear budget constraint, will assure generality. One such

---

[5]This holds for any system of demand functions whose domain is:

$$(p_1, \ldots, p_n, M) \mid \left[M - \sum_{k=1}^{n} \gamma_k p_k \right] > 0.$$

for a rigorous proof the interested reader is referred to Seo (1973)

function as is shown by Basmann, Molina and Slottje (1983, 1984b), is
the Generalized Fechner–Thurstone (GFT) direct utility function:

$$U(X;\theta) = \prod_{i=1}^{n}(X_i - \gamma_i)^{\theta_i},$$ (1.4)

where:

$$X_i > \max\{0,\gamma_i\},$$ (1.5)
$$\theta_i = \theta_i^*(p,M;\Psi)e^{u_i} > 0, \quad i=1,2,\ldots,n,$$
$$\theta = \sum_{i=1}^{n}\theta_i$$

The n-tuple θ of positive valued functions $\theta_i(p,M;\Psi)$ for $i=1,2,\ldots,n$,
represents the parameter of $U(X;\theta)$.[6] The traditional distinction between
parameters and arguments is assumed.[7] The vector $u = (u_1,u_2,\ldots,u_n)$ is
a latent random vector with zero mean vector and finite positive definite
variance matrix Λ_0, and represents stochastic changes of tastes. Serial
covariance matrices Λ_k, , $k = 1,2,\ldots,K$, may represent persistence of
those stochastic changes. The vector $\Psi = (\psi_1,\psi_2,\ldots,\psi_r)$ of observable
non-stochastic variables, other than current p and M, represents other
systematic taste changers.

It is easy to show that maximization of (1.4) subject to (1.1) above
yields the following demand function:

$$x_i^* = \frac{\theta_i(p,M;\Psi)}{\theta(p,M;\Psi)p_i}\left[M - \sum_{k=1}^{n}\gamma_k p_k\right] + \gamma_i \quad i=1,2,\ldots,n$$ (1.6)

---

[6]In actual econometric applications the exponent functions θ_i are assumed to depend
also on a random variable u_i in accordance with a general theory of stochastic changes
of consumer taste (Basmann, 1985). The theorems presented in this note are unaffected
by the presence or absence of the random variables in the exponent functions θ_i. In
other words, the theorems are true even in microtheory contexts, where interest in the
likelihood of hypotheses is absent.

[7]Basmann and Slottje (1987) write: *The vector X of quantities is the only* argument *of
the GFT direct utility function (1.4), p, M, Ψ and u_i are parameters of (1.4). ... In terms
of economic behavior, the argument X is under the consumer groups' control, whereas
the parameters are not. We assume here that the consumer group does not choose prices
and its total expenditure is exogenous.*

which is in the form of (1.3) above, implying that every system of demand functions necessarily results in the maximization of a direct utility function of the GFT form.[8] In fact the GFT form is the least restricted algebraic form of direct utility function satisfying the necessary and sufficient conditions for describing the utility maximizing behavior of a consumer (or a group of consumers)[9]. Since the existence of a direct utility function of the GFT form is always implied it can never be rejected as a viable alternative hypothesis on empirical grounds.

In other words, if revealed preference observations satisfy (1), then consumer behavior *necessarily* results in maximization of the GFT direct utility function. This establishes **Theorem 2**.

The GFT direct utility function is designed for intertemporal comparisons of consumer equilibria. Time periods are sufficiently long to allow budget constraints, i. e., prices and total expenditure to change significantly. The fundamental assumption is that periods sufficiently long for such changes to occur are also sufficiently long for significant changes of taste to occur as well. As elsewhere in science, this kind of correlation does not entail that budget constraint changes "cause" or produce the accompanying taste changes.

The GFT direct utility function, however, does not imply that the intratemporal indifference maps are of the Cobb-Douglas form. Basmann, Molina, and Slottje (1983) stressed the point with an important counterexample. Nor, of course, does the GFT direct utility function imply that intratemporal indifference maps are homothetic. On the other hand, the GFT direct utility function does not exclude the possibility that intratemporal or static indifference maps are homothetic, or even Cobb-Douglas in form. Being applied to data that cannot in principle test such hypotheses as the latter, GFT theory makes no assertion about forms of static indifference maps or preferences.

It is emphasized that satisfaction of the strong or weak axioms of revealed preference is not necessary for the above results to hold. Suppose however that it is possible to infer from S a strictly neoclassical direct utility function $V(X; \psi)$ that rationalizes S in the sense that to each observation in S it assigns the demand elasticities $E_{ij}(p, M)$ $i, j = 1, \ldots, n$.

---

[8]Seo (1973) showed the GFT would generalize consumer behavior even when all of the traditional properties of the demand functions do not hold.

[9]See Basmann, Molina and Slottje (1983, 1984b)

The criterion of closeness of fit to the revealed preference data in S is embedded in the algorithm, of course. Under that criterion, the GFT direct utility function and some neoclassical direct utility function $V(X; \psi)$ just described are equally well-supported by the empirical data.[10]

One use of the notion of a strictly neoclassical direct utility function is to define the mathematical characteristics, we should expect a system of demand functions to possess in case variations of the budget constraint have absolutely no effect on consumer tastes. Probably that is the most widespread use of utility functions, but it is not potentially the most important use. A number of policy-relevant concepts and measurements necessarily presuppose specification of a direct utility function.

The empirical rationale for calculating the optimality of a policy – relevant measurement or program based on a given utility function (say) $V(X; \psi)$ is that $V(X; \psi)$ rationalizes relevant historical data batches like S.[11]

However, the optimality, of a policy-relevant measurement or program rationalized by $V(X; \psi)$ is not unique on the relevant data. The data will always afford at least equal rationale for basing the policy-relevant measurement or program on the GFT form. The following examples, chosen for their timeliness, suffice to illustrate the point: TCLIs, or "true"-cost-of-living indexes (Konyus, 1924; 1936; Fisher and Shell, 1968, pp. 97-101), are defined in terms of a presupposed direct utility function. You cannot calculate a Konyus-Fisher-Shell TCLI without specifying a form of direct utility function.[12] A COLA (cost-of-living adjustment) schedule for increasing salaries and pensions of (say) federal employees might be prescribed in terms of increasing salaries and pensions of (say) federal employees might be prescribed in terms of a TCLI based on a direct utility function $V(X; \psi)$. For sake of illustration, suppose that a Leontief form of $V(X; \psi)$ is supported by "real-world" historical data on federal employees' revealed tastes. Then the modified Laspeyres forms of price-indexes

---

[10]A method of determining the exponents θ_i in (2a-b) in terms of $V(X; \psi)$ is described by (Basmann et al., 1983, p. 412); see also (Basmann *et al.*, 1985a, pp. 17-20).

[11]To a specified degree of approximation, of course.

[12]A computer algorithm may chose a form for you without revealing the chosen form to you, however. Nor would it be a simple matter for you to recover the implicit form chosen by the algorithm. As a result, analysis of the sensitivity of the algorithmic TCLI to changes in (say) prices, income, and other economic factors would become impracticable.

currently in official use can validly be regarded as (approximate) TCLIs. However, there would necessarily be at least two other TCLIs equally as well-supported as the CPI (Consumer Price Index) formula by the same historical data, and equally entitled to consideration as a basis for COLAs. If the alternative TCLI based on the GFT direct utility function were to be adopted, the stream of COLA payments would differ in timing and amount from that rationalized by the TCLI based on $V(X;\psi)$.[13] Examining all TCLIs equally well-supported by empirical data is needed.[14] Examination of observationally equivalent alternatives can throw considerable light on some questions already raised in the policy process, e.g., such as whether (say) COLAs tied to the CPI under-compensate Social Security recipients and overcompensate (say) federal employees and pensioners. We discuss these problems fully in chapter four.

Where it is recognized, the nontestability of a strictly neoclassical direct utility function against the GFT form, even with flawless revealed preference data, is not a serious problem for economic analysis and econometrics. To begin with, it is not a technical problem or puzzle for either pure economic theory or econometrics. Given the sample data S, estimation of the GFT form puts the smallest premium on assuming greater knowledge than one actually has. The GFT direct utility function will afford the closest fit to S. That does not mean that it is the "best" choice on which to base a policy, but it is a sound reason for not ruling it out in advance. If a strictly neoclassical $V(X;\psi)$ — for instance, a direct implicit addilog form (Barnett, 1981, pp. 262-267) — fits a sample S almost as well as the GFT,[15] the different policies that would be optimal under $V(X;\psi)$ and under the GFT form respectively can be described, analyzed, and disseminated to participants in the policy process to the extent resources allow. Where practical policy measures are to be based on the choice of direct utility function, that choice is inherently political,

---

[13]The authors' forecast of the 1984 TCLI based on (2) below is about 8% lower than the projected CPI-U.

[14]Once an agency such as the Bureau of Labor Statistics has collected and prepared the data for computation of CPI-U or CPI-W, the additional cost of computing alternative TCLIs based on (2a-b) is negligible (relatively).

[15]It is possible that the neoclassical direct utility function might fit equally as well as (2a-b) - (3a-c). Easily arranged in a simulation (not Monte Carlo!) experiment (Basmann et al. 1985a; 1985b), the actual occurrence of such an event appears unlikely with "real-world" time-series and cross-section data.

not scientific, as a consequence of the empirical nontestability described
above.

The problem is chiefly one of exerting professional responsibility towards participants in the policy process. The illustration above, involving
the alternative COLA programs that would be optimal under the GFT
form and some alternative $V(X; \psi)$, respectively, suffices to emphasize the
point. Other illustrations from applied economics will be discussed in this
book. No sample S of data can afford an objective basis for choosing (say)
measures of consumer surplus, compensating variation, or equivalent variation based on (say) $V(X; \psi)$ rather than the GFT form, or conversely.
Mainstream tradition has treated nontestability of "seemingly alternative" economic hypotheses as matters for philosophers' concern rather
than economists'. A consequence is that even major works on welfare
economics fail to mention the empirical nonuniqueness of the most basic
concept of that field, e.g., Harberger, 1971, p. 788; McKenzie, 1983, p. 3.
In chapter three, we further define the GFT and its properties and discuss
its ability to indicate Veblen effects in relation to fixed preference forms
that can't. Chapter four presents an example of the GFT's relevance for
true cost-of-living indices and chapter five presents cross country comparisons of preference variation. Chapter six discusses a new model of habit
persistance and chapter seven concludes the book.

Chapter 2

The GFT Utility Function

2.1 Background and History

Samuelson, in his Foundations of Economic Analysis (1947), credits Walras with having shown many years before that it is possible to modify utility analysis so as to take account of the peculiar properties of money; (Samuelson, 1947b, p. 118).The first part of this chapter is adapted in part from Basmann, Molina and Slottje (1987). The latter exposition follows Basmann, Molina and Slottje (1984a). In response to Walras' critics who feared "that there was something viciously circular in assuming the existence of prices and of a 'value for money' in the midst of the process by which that value was to be determined" Samuelson sought to clear up such misconceptions, by deriving the consumer's demand function for holding of money from a utility function subject to a linear budget constraint in which the price of "gold"[1] and the rate of interest, as well as commodity prices and total expenditure appear as parameters; (Samuelson, 1947b, pp. 119-121). Samuelson introduced commodity prices and the price of "gold" into the consumer's ordinal direct utility function $U(X; p)$ as parameters.[2]

---

[1] "Of course no reader will think that I attach any particular importance to gold or any other metal; any conventional unit which serves as money will do." (Samuelson, 1947b, p. 119).

[2] X designates the vector $(X_1, \ldots, X_n)$ and is confined to the positive n-orthant, X_i designates quantity of the ith commodity, p is the vector $(p_1, \ldots, p_n)$ of positive commodity prices. The semi-colon is used to separate the argument of a function from its parameters. M designates total expenditure.

Apart from the usual restrictions on fixed-preference utility functions, only homogeneity of degree zero in all prices was imposed. Even without an explicit form of a direct utility function that restriction is sufficient to imply the meaningful, refutable hypothesis that the demand for (holding) money has unitary own-price elasticity; (Samuelson, 1947b, p. 121).

Thus in small compass Samuelson laid out the schematic framework for the theory of price-dependent direct utility functions, which – as he mentioned – had much broader theoretical and empirical scope than rationalization of consumer demand for holding money. In that connection, Samuelson mentioned the need to introduce prices into indifference loci in the case of commodities that are valued for their exclusiveness so that preferences are altered by changes in their relative prices;[3] (Samuelson, 1947b, p. 119). Another kind of case (not mentioned by Samuelson) calling for the introduction of market prices, or some other kind of preference-changing parameters,[4] into direct utility functions occurs in connection with the

---

[3]*E.g.*, precious stones, gold (possibly) have been considered as "conspicuous consumption" goods, the purchase of which acquire greater or less snob appeal accordingly as their prices increase or decrease. Thorstein Veblen (1899) is usually cited in this connection. Veblen (1899) put forward an explanatory theory of the utility of commodities that attempts to account for the formation and change of consumer preferences over time. Actually, the utility of commodities is viewed as a resultant of two kinds of utility, which compete with each other in affecting the consumers' responses to changes in prices consumers must pay and to the consumers' abilities to pay, i.e., the total expenditure of which a consumer is capable (Veblen, 1899, pp. 97-99). In the present connection it must be emphasized that Veblen considered this secondary utility of commodities to be pervasive rather than confined to a few unusual commodities (Veblen, 1899, p. 101). According to Veblen, consumption goods, even productive goods, generally possess and exhibit a mixture of primary and secondary utility. Later in the chapter "Pecuniary Cannons of Taste", Veblen suggests that there are no goods supplied in any trade which do not have secondary utility in greater or less degree (Veblen, 1899, p. 157). According to Veblen's theory, conspicuous consumption, or the consumption of goods and services that is motivated predominantly by secondary utility, is not confined to the leisure class but prevails over all the social and income classes from richest to poorest (Veblen, 1899, pp. 88-85, p. 103). This brief review of Veblen's theory of the utility of commodities makes clear the practical motive for assuming that prices and total expenditures have some influence on the parameters of a direct utility function that is supposed to be mathematical description of the resultant effects of primary and secondary utility in Veblen's sense.

[4]In empirical demand analysis and predetermined variable, apart from prices p and total expenditure M as arguments, is *ipso facto* hypothesized to be a preference-changing parameter in relation to the underlying preference structure, *e.g*, time as a trend variable,

wide use and robustness of double logarithmic demand and expenditure-share functions in empirical demand analysis. For sound reasons, the double logarithmic form has been popular with empirical demand analysis, chiefly because it is linear in the elasticity coefficients that are to be estimated, and the attendant certainty about the statistical properties of least squares elasticity estimators under the stochastic assumptions usually made. On the other hand, it has long been known that interpretation of the raw elasticities of such a complete system of "demand functions" as the price and total expenditure elasticities of demand is inconsistent with the theory of utility-maximizing consumer; (Schultz, 1938; pp. 628-633; Battalio, et. al., 1973, esp. p. 366). Of course, for some specified, definite form of the underlying direct utility function, the known forms of derived demand functions or expenditure-share functions might happen to imply that

1. they possess logarithmic Taylor expansions at some point $(\ln p^0, \ln M^0)$ of interest

2. that the derived demand functions or expenditure-share functions can be computed from their Taylor expansions, and

3. that the remainder R_2 after the linear terms is sufficiently small.

Condition (2) does not necessarily follow from condition (1) so it really isn't sound practice merely to assume that the double logarithmic "demand" functions or expenditure-share functions afford local approximations to the derived demand functions or derived expenditure-share functions when the theoretical forms of the latter are unknown. The Taylor approximation has to be rationalized by the known form of the function it is to approximate.[5] However, specification of definite, explicit forms of direct utility functions that are dependent on market prices, or on other preference- changing variables such as total expenditure, can yield meaningful alternative rationalizations of systems of double-logarithmic

---

or "dummy variables" to change intercepts (Basmann, 1956, p. 48).

  [5]For instance consider $f(X) = \exp(-1/X^2)$ at $x \neq 0$, $f(0) = 0$. The function possesses continuous derivatives of all orders; consequently, the Taylor expansion exists. No matter to how many terms the Taylor expansion is carried, the remainder R_n is equal to the value of $f(X)$ itself. *cf.* Franklin (1940), p. 150.

demand function approximations and expenditure-share function approximations. Fixed-preference utility function cannot explain why empirical double logarithmic demand functions and expenditure-share functions do as well as they often do in practice.

Samuelson's brief note on the demand for money attracted little response at the time. Economists concerned with analysis of variable preferences and causes of changes in taste tended to put greater emphasis on social and technological factors, habit persistence (Duesenberry, 1949), advertising and other forms of selling effort, income and parameters of the income distribution (Johnson, 1952), than on changes in market prices. Ichimura (1951) and Tintner (1952) defined changes in preferences as changes in the form of the ordinal utility function or indifference map and derived the corresponding shifts in demand as linear combinations of Slutsky-Hicks terms (Basmann, 1954, 1955). Tintner (1960, p. 109) was concerned with interdependence of consumer's utility functions; he considered the case of direct utility functions that incorporate as parameters the incomes of all individuals in society, including the consumer's own, i.e. the utility function is dependent on the empirical income distribution. In the same paper, Tintner also considered the case of direct utility functions that include the quantities of all commodities consumed by all other individual consumers (Tintner, 1960, pp. 110-112).

Subsequent writers on price-dependent utility functions seldom mention Samuelson's contribution specifically. Kalman (1968), Dusansky and Kalman (1972; 1974), Clower and Riley (1976), Wichers (1976), were concerned primarily with demand functions that are not homogeneous of degree zero in all prices and money income, i.e., with the presence of "money illusion".

The question of whether the absence of zero degree homogeneity in the above demand functions alone can exhaust the meaning of "money illusion" is still open and interesting, especially in reference to the representative consumer in statistical demand analysis (Schultz, 1938, esp. p. 630)[6] but it need not detain us here. There are other motivations, both

----

[6]The fact that empirical per capita demand functions show "money illusion", in this sense does not imply that any of the individual consumer demand functions are not homogeneous of degree zero in average market prices and per capita total expenditure. Per capita money illusion may be accounted for as a property of the distribution of prices paid and of total expenditure.

traditional and recent for extending Samuelson's schematic framework for
a theory of price-dependent preferences. Kalman (1968, p. 497) mentions
the Veblen effect, or snob appeal and the Scitovsky hypothesis that consumers often consider commodity prices and commodity price changes as
indicators of quality and quality changes (Scitovsky, 1945, p. 100).

R. A. Pollak (1977) has provided some additional important and empirically meaningful interpretations of price dependent preferences. This
book is concerned with Pollak's interpretations and with further empirically meaningful interpretations of our own. In Sec. III of his article
Pollak (1977) offers two alternative interpretations of price- dependent
preferences and discusses the implications of price-dependent preferences
for welfare economics. He distinguishes two models of price- dependent
preferences:

1. in which the objects of choice are commodity bundles and the ordering is dependent on prices

2. in which the objects of choice are "quantity-price situations". (Pollak, 1977, p. 65, p. 74)

In Pollak's notation, n-vector P^N and P^M designate "normal prices"
and market prices respectively. Pollak considers two types of demand
functions:

1. market price (MP) demand functions $Q = h(P^M, \mu; P^N)$ are found
   by maximizing the price dependent utility function under the usual
   budget constraint with $P^M Q = \mu$, where μ denotes total expenditure;

2. the normal price (NP) demand functions show the consumption pattern implied by the MP demand functions when $P^N = P^M$, *i.e.*
   $Q = h(P^M, \mu; P^N)$. *cf.* Pollak (1977, p. 66).

Pollak's NP demand functions are identical with what we shall call (sim-
ply) individual consumer's market demand functions; the latter constitute
the subject matter intersection between his article and the present book.

Although economists have long been receptive to the notion that consumer preferences vary systematically in response to past consumption,

advertising effort, and product innovation,[7] there has been considerable
reluctance to consider changes in income and market prices as potentially
important preference-changing variables. This may be, as Scitovsky (1945,
p. 100) put it, because of "fearing the havoc it may wreak with the whole
theory of choice." Pollak (1978) distinguishes two very different motivations for economists' reluctance to formulate and test hypotheses about
preference formation and preference variation. In a nutshell, the first of
the motivations is that preference- and taste-formation are none of the
economists' business.[8] The second is a widely held, but rather vaguely expressed, notion that "if you let preferences vary, then you can make your
system of demand functions fit any empirical data whatsoever." It seems
to be believed that the introduction of the hypothesis that individual consumer's preferences vary with respect to official or market prices somehow
constitutes an unwarranted rescue of utility analysis from empirical refutation; Pollak cites Stigler and Becker (1977, esp. pp. 78-79) as representing
an extreme position on the formulation and testing of variable preference
hypotheses (Pollak, 1978, p. 375). However, Stigler and Becker (1977) appear to be rescuing fixed preference theory and interpersonal uniformity
of preferences from empirical refutation by using household production
theory as a catch-all.

Fear that price-dependent preferences will wreak havoc with the theory
of choice, with traditional or "new" welfare economics, or with household
production theory is real, to be sure, but it is unfounded. This is most
clearly demonstrated in the case where consumer demand functions

1. possess the Slutsky property,[9]

2. are rationalized by a definite, explicit price-dependent direct utility

---

[7] cf. Report of Kiel Meeting, *Econometrica*, Vol. 24, pp. 327-328.

[8] On this, see Pollak's (1978) quotation from Friedman's textbook Friedman (1962).

[9] A system of demand functions $X(p, M)$ is said to possess the Slutsky property if and
only if the Slutsky derivatives K_{ij}^* satisfy the following conditions:

$$K_{ij}^* = K_{ji}^*$$
$$K_{ii}^* < 0$$
$$\sum_{i=1}^{n} p_j K_{ij}^* = 0$$

and the matrix $[K_{ij}^*]$ is p.s.d., where K_{ij}^* is defined in terms of demand functions function $U(X; p)$

3. are also rationalized by an equally definite, explicitly stated fixed preference direct utility function $V(X)$.

Where $U(X; p)$ and $V(X)$ are explicitly stated, they are empirically meaningful alternative hypotheses in Samuelson's sense (Samuelson, 1947, p. 121).

In his article, Robert Pollak (1977, pp. 65, 69, 73) argues correctly that a system of Slutsky-Hicks demand functions derived from a price-dependent preference ordering can sometimes also be derived from another preference ordering that is independent of prices. Pollak instantiates his argument by describing a Klein-Rubin direct utility function in which the lower terminal parameters depend on prices in an explicit form; he argues that the implied Slutsky-Hicks demand functions can also be derived from an alternative preference ordering that does not depend on prices, namely, a preference ordering that corresponds to the indirect utility function $\psi(P, \mu; P^N)$; Pollak (1977, p. 70) demonstrated coexistence of two distinct direct utility functions yielding the same Slutsky-Hicks demand functions poses an exceptionally important interpretative problem for the theory of individual consumer behavior. (Here we suppose, of course, that the demand functions in question agree closely with, or fit, some individual consumer's quantity-price-total expenditure data.) To begin with the formal distinction between the underlying price-dependent utility function $U(X; p)$, on the one hand, and the simultaneously underlying price-independent utility function $V(X)$ on the other, if the latter exists, it is empirically detectable, therefore meaningful. Moreover, the difference is feasibly detectable in practice by current techniques of behavioral economics when used in conjunction with revealed preference techniques, but not by revealed preferences alone.

X_j^*, $\quad j = 1, 2, \ldots, n$ by

$$K_{ij}^* = \frac{\partial X_i^*}{\partial p_j} + X_j^* \frac{\partial X_i^*}{\partial M}$$

2.2   Least Restricted Direct Utility Function

Given that every system $X(M,p)$ of demand functions whatsoever that satisfy the budget constraint (1.1) can be expressed in the form (1.3) (as noted in chapter one), the following question naturally arises: What is the most robust, or least restricted, form of direct utility function that can rationalize demand functions (1.3)? The question is an extremely important one because its answer defines the natural scientific boundaries of a theory of the utility-maximizing consumer. Special, restricted forms (or algorithms) for direct utility functions imply "straightjackets on the facts," to borrow a term from Samuelson (1947, p. 88) which permit such restricted forms to be disconfirmed in principle, at least, by empirical data. Their potential empirical disconfirmation makes such restricted direct utility functions unsuitable for use in defining boundaries of a theory of the utility-maximizing consumer, especially where the theory is expected to have policy relevance, e.g., in the construction of cost-of- living indexes.

It turns out that the direct utility function characterized by (2.1), below, rationalizes every system of demand functions that satisfy the budget constraint (1.1). The GFT form of direct utility function with argument X is defined by

$$U(X;\theta) \;=\; \prod_{i=1}^{n}(X_i - \gamma_i)^{\theta_i(\alpha)} \tag{2.1}$$

$X_i \geq \max(0,\gamma_i)$. The n-tuple θ of positive valued functions $\theta_i(\alpha)$, for $i = 1,2,\ldots,n$, is (said to be) the parameter of $U(X;\theta)$. The notational device of separating the argument parameter of a function by a semicolon will be used throughout this study whenever it is essential to distinguish between them. The GFT direct utility function (2.1) looks superficially like the Stone-Geary and Cobb-Douglas direct utility function, the latter being, from the formal point of view at least, highly restricted special cases of (2.1). First- and second-order partial derivatives of (2.1) with respect to elements of X will be designated by $U_i(X;\theta)$ and $U_{ij}(X;\theta)$, respectively, or, as is usually done, by U_i and U_{ij}. The marginal rate of substitution of commodity k for commodity i at a point X of the domain in (2.1) is defined by

$$R_i^{(k)}(X;\alpha) =_{df} \frac{U_i(X;\theta)}{U_k(X;\theta)} \tag{2.2}$$

$$= \frac{\theta_i(\alpha)\,(X_k - \gamma_k)}{\theta_k(\alpha)\,(X_i - \gamma_i)} \tag{2.3}$$

The preference field, or system of indifference surfaces determined by (2.1), remains invariant against the replacement of (2.1) by any monotonically increasing function of $U(X;\theta)$ (see Hicks, 1946, pp. 306-307).

In aggregating individual consumer's utility functions we find it very convenient to use the following replacement of $U(X;\theta)$ by another GFT direct utility function $U(X;\vartheta)$:

$$\theta(\alpha) =_{df} \sum_{i=1}^{n} \theta_i(\alpha). \tag{2.4}$$

The new parameter ϑ is required to satisfy the condition

$$\sum_{i=1}^{n} \vartheta_i(\alpha) = \vartheta. \tag{2.5}$$

where the numerical value of ϑ is specified. This requirement is satisfied by the definition

$$U(X;\vartheta) = [U(X;\vartheta)]^{\frac{\vartheta}{\theta}} \tag{2.6}$$

$$= \prod_{i=1}^{n} (X_i - \gamma_i)^{\vartheta_i(\alpha)}. \tag{2.7}$$

From (2.1) and (2.6-2.7) it follows that

$$\vartheta_i(\alpha) = \frac{\theta_i(\alpha)\vartheta}{\theta}, \quad i = 1, 2, \ldots, n. \tag{2.8}$$

Consequently, for every X in the domain (2.1), $R_i^{(k)}$ the *marginal rate of substitution of commodity k for commodity i*, remains invariant:

$$R_i^{(k)}(X;\vartheta) =_{df} \frac{U_i(X;\vartheta)}{U_k(X;\vartheta)} \tag{2.9}$$

$$= R_i^{(k)}(X;\vartheta) \tag{2.10}$$

at every point X of the domain (2.1).

In view of this invariance of preference maps defined by GFT direct utility functions we are able validly to specify that for every pair of distinct individual consumers μ and ν, the parameters $\vartheta^{(\mu)}$ and $\vartheta^{(\nu)}$ satisfy the condition

$$\sum_{i=1}^{n} \vartheta^{(\mu)}(\alpha) = \sum_{i=1}^{n} \vartheta^{(\nu)}(\alpha). \tag{2.11}$$

This respecification does not involve any interpersonal comparison of utility or levels of satisfaction.

In the next section the theory of the utility-maximizing consumer will be linked up with a theoretical representation of the personal multivariate distribution of expenditures on commodities and components of income and wealth. This linkage will be found to destroy the ordinal character of utility as far as the combined theory is concerned. It will remain true, of course, that preference fields will be invariant against replacement of (2.6-2.7) by a monotonically increasing function of itself. However, such a replacement of (2.6-2.7) will imply empirically testable changes in measures of inequality in the personal distributions of expenditures on commodities and components of income and wealth. The parameter ϑ, which is a parameter of every individual consumer's direct utility function, turns out to be an inequality parameter of the personal distribution of income. A ceteris paribus increase of ϑ causes an increase in, e.g., the Gini measure of income inequality. Consequently the values of the parameters ϑ_i, for $i = 1, 2, \ldots, n$, in (2.7) cannot be changed arbitrarily as they can with purely ordinal utility functions.

The direct utility function (2.1) is a straightforward generalization of an experimentally interpreted direct utility function first introduced by the experimental psychologist L. L. Thurstone in his well-known article *"The Indifference Function"* (1931). What economists call a direct utility function is some monotonically increasing function or other of what Thurstone referred to as a *satisfaction curve*. In order to write an equation for this *satisfaction curve*, Thurstone (1931, pp. 141-42) laid down five psychological assumptions. The fifth assumption was that motivation, i.e., the slope of the *satisfaction curve* in the direction of increasing X_i, is inversely proportional to the amount X_i already possessed,[10] which is G.

---

[10]Thurstone (1931, p.141) states that motivation is equivalent to the economists

T. Fechner's proffered psychophysical law, or universalization, of a well-known empirical regularity discovered by E. H. Weber: *The increase of a stimulus to produce a given increase of sensation bears a constant ratio to the total stimulus* (see James, 1890, reprint 1950, pp. 539-548). According to Thurstone, the psychological hypothesis that led him to use the Fechner "law" fit the experimental data better than other hypotheses that were tried.[11] Consequently he proffered the special case of the form (2.1) with the parameters θ_i fixed.[12] Aware of the arbitrariness of the choice of the origin of the domain γ,[13] Thurstone used $\gamma = 0$.[14]

2.3 Nonvacuous Preference Changers

The components of α, are called *nonvacuous preference changers*. These are classified under two main heads:

1. preference changers that are *systematic and observable*, and

2. preference changers that are *stochastic and unobservable*.

In order to define the term "nonvacuous" we consider some elementary geometry of the preference field defined by the *Fechner-Thurstone* direct utility function (2.1).

In order to define nonvacuous preference changers the cofactors of elements of the bordered Hessian of partial derivatives of direct utility functions must first be derived. Let $|U|$ be the bordered Hessian for (2.6-2.7). We have

$$|U| = \frac{(-1)^n [U(X;\theta)]^{n+1} \left(\prod_{k=1}^n \theta_k\right) \left(\sum_{k=1}^n \theta_k\right)}{\prod_{k=1}^n (X_k - \gamma_k)^2} \tag{2.12}$$

The magnitude of the cofactor of U_{ii} in $|U|$ at the point X is determined by

$$\frac{|U_{ii}|}{|U|} = \frac{-(\theta - \theta_i)(X_i - \gamma_i)^2}{\theta_i \theta [U(X;\theta)]} \tag{2.13}$$

"marginal utility."

[11]See Thurstone, 1931, pp. 142-143)
[12]*ibid.* (p.147)
[13]*ibid.* (p.142)
[14]*ibid.* (p.141)

The magnitude of the cofactor of U_{ij}, for $i \neq j$, in $|U|$ at the point X is determined by (2.12) and

$$\frac{|U_{ij}|}{|U|} = \frac{(X_i - \gamma_i)(X_j - \gamma_j)}{\theta \left[U(X; \theta) \right]} \qquad (2.14)$$

Finally, the magnitude of the cofactor of U_i in $|U|$ at the point X is determined by

$$\frac{|U_{i0}|}{|U|} = \frac{(X_i - \gamma_i)}{\theta \left[U(X; \theta) \right]} \qquad (2.15)$$

Let X^0 designate any given point of the domain (2.1). Let $S(X^0, \theta)$ be the set of points satisfying

$$U(X; \theta) = U(X^0; \theta). \qquad (2.16)$$

Here $S(X^0; \theta)$ is the indifference hypersurface passing through X^0. Let

$$q^0 - \sum_{k=1}^{n} X_k^0 \cos \phi_k = 0, \quad 0 \leq \phi_k < \frac{\pi}{2}, \qquad (2.17)$$

be the equation of the hyperplane tangent to $S(X^0; \theta)$ at X^0. Finally let the real number λ^0 be defined at the point X^0 by

$$\lambda^0 = \theta \left[U(X^0; \theta) \right] \left[q^0 - \sum_{k=1}^{n} \gamma_k \cos \phi_k \right]^{-1}, \qquad (2.18)$$

We define S_{ii}, S_{ij}, and S_{i0} at X^0 in domain (2.1) by

$$S_{ii} = \lambda^0 \frac{|U_{ii}|}{|U|} \qquad (2.19)$$

$$= \frac{-(\theta - \theta_i)(X_i^0 - \gamma_i)^2 \left[q^0 - \sum_{k=1}^{n} \gamma_k \cos \phi_k \right]^{-1}}{\theta_i}; \qquad (2.20)$$

$$S_{ij} = \lambda^0 \frac{|U_{ij}|}{|U|} \qquad (2.21)$$

$$= (X_i^0 - \gamma_i)(X_j^0 - \gamma_j) \left[q^0 - \sum_{k=1}^{n} \gamma_k \cos \phi_k \right]^{-1}; \qquad (2.22)$$

and

$$S_{i0} = \lambda^0 \frac{|U_{i0}|}{|U|} \tag{2.23}$$

$$= (X_i^0 - \gamma_i) \left[q^0 - \sum_{k=1}^{n} \gamma_k \cos \phi_k \right]^{-1}. \tag{2.24}$$

The functions S_{ij}, for $i, j = 1, 2, \ldots, n$, form a symmetric negative semidefinite matrix; and

$$\sum_{j=1}^{n} S_{ij} \cos \phi_j = 0, \tag{2.25}$$

$$\sum_{j=1}^{n} S_{ij} \cos \phi_i = 0. \tag{2.26}$$

The functions S_{ij} look like *Slutsky-Hicks substitution terms*.[15] However, Eq. (2.17) describes any tangent hyperplane, not necessarily a budget hyperplane. In the special case of a budget hyperplane the expressions S_{ij} do, indeed, reduce to the ordinary Slutsky-Hicks substitution terms *defined in terms* of *direct utility functions*; S_{i0} reduces to the ordinary income term defined in terms of direct utility functions.[16] We shall refer to S_{i0} as the substitution term proper (to the direct utility function) and to S_{i0} as the expansion term proper (to the direct utility function). We are now in position to define the concept of a nonvacuous preference changer.

A component α_h of α is (said to be) a *nonvacuous preference changer* with respect to the direct utility function $U(X; \theta)$ if, and only if, for at least one point X^0 of the domain (2.1) a change in α_h causes a change in at least one of the expansion terms proper, S_{i0}, for $i, j = 1, 2, \ldots, n$, at X^0. Notice that this concept of a *nonvacuous preference changer* is always defined relative to a specified direct utility function.

Alternatively, and equivalently, a component α_h of α is (said to be) a *nonvacuous preference changer* with respect to $U(X; \theta)$ if, and only if, for at least one point X^0 of the domain (2.1) a change in α_h causes a change in at least one marginal rate of substitution $R_i^{(k)}(X; \theta)$ at X^0; illustrated in (2.9-2.10) (*cf.* Ichimura, 1951; also Tintner, 1952; Basmann, 1955, 1956).

---

[15]See Hicks, 1946, pp. 309-310
[16]See Hicks, 1946, p. 309

The concept of *nonvacuous preference changer* (as defined above) will be exemplified many times in the sections that follow.

2.4   Demand Functions

In this section, let p be interpreted as a vector of budget constraint prices while M is the total expenditure on commodities X_i where $i = 1, 2, \ldots, n$. The consumer is assumed to select a definite equilibrium n-tuple $(X_1^*, \ldots, X_n^*)$ such that the direct utility function (2.6-2.7) is maximized subject to the budget constraint (1.1). Equation (2.1) is said to be a constraint because (as is usually assumed in the theory of consumer demand for one reason or other) the consumer does not treat M and p as choice variables in this optimization process.

As was shown in Chapter 1, the derived demand functions are expressed by

$$X_i^* = \frac{\theta_i(\alpha)p_i^{-1}}{\sum_{k=1}^{n} \theta_k(\alpha)} \left[M - \sum_{k=1}^{n} \gamma_k p_k \right] + \gamma_i, \quad i = 1, 2, \ldots, n. \qquad (2.27)$$

Which has the form (1.3) as was previously shown. Since every system of demand functions can be represented in the form (1.3), it follows that every system of demand functions can be derived from the GFT direct utility function (2.1). This assures us that, in accord with the principle of Occam's razor, the GFT form of direct utility function does not embody any excessively restrictive assumptions about maximizing behavior of consumers.

The consumer demand depends on, and only on, the parameters of the specified Fechner-Thurstone direct utility function $U(X; \theta)$ and the parameters of the budget constraint (1.1).

The economic theorists' concern with the Giffen paradox of Hicks (1946, p.35), with the possible existence of *inferior goods* and *nonlinearity* of Engel curves, the interrelatedness of goods in consumption, i.e., their substitutability and complementarity (Hicks, 1946, Chap. III), and with shifts in demand (Ichimura, 1951; Tintner, 1952; Basmann, 1954-55,1956), make those topics matters of concern to the econometrician involved in estimating (and testing hypotheses about) the parameters of systems of demand functions. Definitions of the above concepts are usually stated in terms of partial derivatives of demand functions. Since the derived demand functions (2.27) allow for the possibility of total expenditure M and budget constraint prices being systematic preference changers, definitions of "inferior good," "Giffen good," "substitutability," and "complementarity" need restatement in order to avoid an otherwise unsuspected change of their usual meanings in use.

Let y be any real variable. The partial derivative of X_i^* with respect to y is formally expressed by

$$\frac{\partial X_i^*}{\partial y} = \frac{\theta_i(\alpha)}{\sum_{k=1}^{n} \theta_k(\alpha)} \frac{\partial}{\partial y} \left[P_i^{-1} \left[M - \sum_{k=1}^{n} \gamma_k p_k \right] \right]$$

$$+ \ p_i^{-1} \left[M - \sum_{k=1}^{n} \gamma_k p_k \right] \left[\sum_{k=1}^{n} \left(\frac{\theta_k}{\theta} \right)^2 \frac{\partial}{\partial y} \left(\frac{\theta_i}{\theta_k} \right) \right],$$

$$i \ = \ 1, 2, \ldots, n. \tag{2.28}$$

In order that the expression (2.28) be nonzero it is necessary that one or more of M, the budget constraint prices p, or one or more elements of α be (specified as) dependent on y.

Stochastic variables are assumed to affect demand functions (2.28) solely by way of the parameters $\theta_i(\alpha)$. Random variables will not be "tacked on" to demand functions, as is traditionally done, in this study. Partial derivatives of X_i^* with respect to M and the budget constraint prices p necessarily satisfy the customary neoclassical restrictions

$$\det[K_{ij}] = 0$$

and

$$K_{ij} = \frac{\partial X_i}{\partial p_j} + X_j \frac{\partial X_i}{\partial M}, \quad i, j, = 1, 2, \ldots, n.$$

Using K_{ij}^* to describe the aforementioned when the functions differentiated are (2.27), we find that the K_{ij}^* are related to substitution terms proper of $U(X; \theta)$ at X^* by the equations

$$K_{ij}^* \ = \ S_{ij} + p_i^{-1} \left[M - \sum_{k=1}^{n} \gamma_k p_k \right] \sum_{k=1}^{n} \left(\frac{\theta_k}{\theta} \right)^2 \left(\frac{\partial}{\partial p_j} + X_j^* \frac{\partial}{\partial M} \right) \frac{\theta_i}{\theta_k},$$

$$i, j \ = \ 1, 2, \ldots, n. \tag{2.29}$$

We shall refer to K_{ij}^* as *apparent substitution terms*. The *apparent income term*, or partial derivative of the demand function with respect to M, is designated by K_{i0}^* and is related to S_{i0}, the *expansion term proper* to $U(X;\theta)$ at X^*, by the equations

$$K_{i0}^* = S_{i0} + p_i^{-1}\left[M - \sum_{k=1}^n \gamma_k p_k\right] \sum_{k=1}^n \left(\frac{\theta_k}{\theta}\right)^2 \frac{\partial}{\partial M}\left(\frac{\theta_i}{\theta_k}\right),$$
$$i = 1,2,\ldots,n. \tag{2.30}$$

Concepts of *inferior good*, *Giffen good*, *substitutability*, and *complementarity* as usually defined tacitly presuppose that the consumers' preferences are not dependent on total expenditure M and/or budget constraint prices, p. This tacit presupposition is an untested assumption about empirical "facts." It is testable in principle but not feasible to test in practice–nor is such testing probably socially desirable even were it to become feasible to do so.[17] Accordingly, we restate all of those definitions with an explicit, much weaker antecedent condition for their use which does not imply that consumers' preferences are independent of the budget constraint parameters:

Conditional Definition 1 *If at a specified point $Q^0 = (M^0, p^0, \alpha^0)$ of the domain of demand functions (2.27), the matrix $\left[K_{ij}^*\right]$ defined by (2.29) is symmetric and negative semidefinite, then:*

1. *commodity i is an* **inferior good** *at Q^0 iff $K_{i0}^* < 0$ at Q^0;*

2. *commodity i is a* **Giffen good** *at Q^0 iff $\frac{\partial X_i^*}{\partial p_i} > 0$ at Q^0;*

3. *commodity j is a* **substitute** *for commodity i at Q^0 iff $j \neq i$ and $K_{i0}^* \geq 0$;*

4. *commodity j is a* **complement** *of commodity i at Q^0 iff $j \neq i$ and $K_{ij}^* < 0$.*

---

[17]It seems amusing that economists since, at the very least, the time of Smiths' infamous *invisible hand*, have been receptive to the notion of the price vector as a market signal yet any readjustment of individual utility extraction technology over time has been a traditional *faux pas*. It is as if the organ which secretes the preferences has been amputated yet somehow still exists *a grin without a cat*. Maybe this is out of the fear of the "havoc it may wreak with the whole theory of choice," as Scitovsky (1945, p.100) stated.

The conditional definition includes as a special case the neoclassical concepts as they are defined under the tacit presupposition that consumers' preferences are independent of total expenditure M and budget constraint prices p. By relaxing the tacit, highly restrictive neoclassical antecedent condition to include a nonempty subclass of demand function systems derived from direct utility functions with parameters that are dependent on total expenditure M and/or budget constraint prices p, we have extended the scope of concepts of an inferior good, a Giffen good, substitutability, and complementarity somewhat. The particular extension of these neoclassical concepts does seem more or less natural in the case of systems of demand functions (2.27) such as Leser-Houthakker additive logarithmic demand functions (see Houthakker, 1960, p. 263), i.e., where $\theta_i = \beta_i M^{\sigma_{i0}} p_i^{-(1+\sigma_{i0})}$, for $i = 1, 2, \ldots, n$, in (2.28), with $\beta_i > 0$, $\beta_1 + \ldots + \beta_n = 1$. Moreover, Arrow (1961, p. 177) has already extended implicitly the neoclassical concepts of "substitutability" and "complementarity" to the K_{ij}^* derived from the additive logarithmic demand functions.[18] However, to extend the scope of those neoclassical terms beyond the class of systems of demand functions characterized by the antecedent condition we set forth would dissolve their neoclassical meaning, lead to no greater understanding of empirical consumer behavior, and (probably) stand in the way of forming more fruitful theoretical concepts out of accumulated experience with systems of empirical demand functions (2.27) derived from the less restricted forms of the GFT direct utility function (2.1).

If α_h is an element of α other than current total expenditure M or a current budget constraint price p, then the derivative of any demand function (2.27) is a *pure Ichimura-Tintner shift in demand*:

$$\frac{\partial X_i^*}{\partial \alpha_h} = p_i^{-1} \left[M - \sum_{k=1}^{n} \gamma_k p_k \right] \left[\sum_{k=1}^{n} \left(\frac{\theta_k}{\theta} \right)^2 \frac{\partial}{\partial \alpha_h} \left(\frac{\theta_i}{\theta_k} \right) \right]$$

$$= -p_k \sum_{j=1}^{n} \sum_{m=1}^{n} \frac{\partial \theta_j}{\partial \alpha_h} \frac{\partial R_m^{(k)}}{\partial \theta_j} S_{ki} \tag{2.31}$$

(see Basmann, 1956, p. 51). Notice that the pure shifts in demand are directly related to the substitution terms S_{ij} proper to the direct utility

---

[18]Arrow (1961, p.177) noted the emptiness of the definition of complementarity: "There is no room for specialized relations of complementarity or substitution among particular pairs of commodities."

function (2.1). Interpretation of pure shifts in demand remains the same as in neoclassical theory.

2.5   Is the GFT a "Flexible Form" ?

Given any system of demand functions that satisfies the ordinary linear budget constraint, the derivation of a direct utility function having the GFT form is straightforward. Basmann *et al.* (1983, p. 412) described how, but the description is short enough to be repeated here. Let $X(p, M; \theta)$ be any system of parametric demand functions that satisfy the ordinary linear budget constraint. There is no other restriction on the choice of demand function system. It may be one of the flexible forms as defined by Diewert,[19] such as the translog (Christensen *et al.*, 1975), the generalized Leontief (Caves and Christensen 1980), the Fourier flexible form (Gallant, 1981), or the minflex Laurent (Barnett, 1983; Barnett, 1985; Barnett *et al.*, 1985). Another rather simple specification that works well with aggregate data expresses the ratios θ_i/θ_k in constant elasticity form, that is, specifies their logarithms as linear functions of logarithms of prices, M and logarithms of other variables assumed to influence the ratios. This specification implies that the logarithmic derivatives $\omega_{i0}^{(k)}$, $\omega_{ij}^{(k)}$, or elasticities of marginal rates of substitution with respect to M, p, or other taste-changing variables (at fixed X) are constant. We shall refer to this specification of $X(p, M; \theta)$ as the constant elasticity of marginal rate of substitution (CEMRS) form.

Regardless of the parametric form of $X(p, M; \theta)$, a GFT direct utility function that rationalizes this system of demand functions can be constructed as follows: Let $K(p, M)$ be any positive-valued function that has partial derivatives at least up to the order of partial derivatives of the demand functions in (2.27) above. Let $X_i(p, M; \theta)$ be the demand function for commodity i. Finally, define the GFT exponent function θ_i by

$$\theta_i = K(p, M) p_i X_i(p, M; \theta), \quad i = 1, 2, \ldots, n. \tag{2.32}$$

The GFT direct utility function with exponents defined by (2.32) necessarily rationalizes the system of demand functions $X(p, M; \theta)$ we started

[19]Diewert (1974) provides the generally accepted definition of a *flexible* functional form: a linearly homogeneous function is flexible if it can provide a second order approximation to an arbitrary twice continuously differentiable linearly homogeneous function.

out with.

2.6 Aggregation of the Utility Function

As its heading indicates, this section is concerned with the representation of per capita (per consumer unit) market demands as magnitudes of consumer demand functions that are derived by constrained maximization of a direct utility function that is a definite aggregation of individual consumer's direct utility functions. Maximization of this aggregate direct utility function is subject to a per capita budget constraint, which itself is an arithmetic average of the individual consumer's budget constraints. In this section attention is confined to the matter of aggregation over a population of individual consumers.

This section emphasizes two practical motives for aggregating individual consumer's GFT direct utility functions into an aggregate direct utility function. The first of these has to do with formulating a specific theoretical connection between individual consumers' preferences, on the one hand, and the personal marginal multivariate distribution of components of received income and components of wealth, on the other. A second practical motive for construction of an aggregate direct utility function is its use in the construction of cost-of-living indexes that can retain meaningfulness even when extended to a population of utility-maximizing individual consumers whose preferences are nonvacuously dependent on total expenditure or one or more budget constraint prices. In particular the aggregate direct utility function is constructed in order to extend the Klein-Rubin approach to constructing a "true cost-of-living" index based on statistical estimates of per capita demand functions (Klein and Rubin, 1947, p. 78).

The need for an extension of the concept of cost of living has been made clear by the record of a half-century of demand analysis. Furthermore, the insufficiency of traditional empirical systems of demand functions to establish that individual consumers' preferences are independent of budget constraint prices and total expenditure severely handicaps the use of indirect utility functions in the construction of cost-of-living indexes in all cases save that originally presented by Klein and Rubin (1947).

From Schultz (1938, pp. 628-633) to Muellbauer (1975), theoretical demand analysts have stressed that "there is, in general, no reason why aggregated market data should obey the same rules as the micro data of any individual, even when, as econometricians usually assume, everyone has the same tastes. Thus the symmetry restrictions do not hold in the aggregate, even if they hold at the micro level" (Muellbauer, 1975, p. 525). An important line of pure theoretical investigation has been concerned with deriving the mathematical consequences (for aggregate demand functions) of the assumption that individual consumers' direct utility functions have preference parameters that are independent of the budget constraint parameters (e.g., see Sonnenschein, 1972, 1973). Other theorists have formulated additional theoretical constraints on individual consumers' direct utility functions that are sufficient to imply deductively that aggregate demand functions satisfy the following conditions:

1. homogeneity of degree zero in prices and income,

2. symmetry of the K_{ij}^* defined previously and

3. negative semidefiniteness of the matrix $[K_{ij}^*]$.

Gorman (1963), Berndt *et al.* (1977), Deaton and Muellbauer (1980a,b), and Jorgenson *et al.* (1982) are representative of that approach. All start from the assumption that, in addition to the assumption that the individual consumers' system of demand functions fall under the assumptions above, the direct utility function actually underlying the demand functions has its parameters independent of total expenditure M and budget constraints prices p. This assumption is, in principle, at least, testable experimentally against the ever-present alternative GFT direct utility function that also rationalizes each individual consumer's system of demand functions. The potential empirical disconfirmation of the fixed preference assumption (embodied in a specified fixed preference direct utility function) affords the fixed preference assumption and the concept of "cost of living" (as equivalent to the "cost of level of utility") their empirical meaningfulness. The alternative GFT direct utility function and the concept of "cost of living" that emerges from it acquire their meaningfulness in precisely the same way: If an incentive-compatible experiment were actually performed, the GFT form $U(X; \theta)$ of direct utility function might well be disconfirmed in favor of a specified fixed preference direct utility function $V(X)$.

The aggregation of individual consumer's GFT direct utility functions involves no "aggregation problem" at all. That is to say, it offers no hope or challenge to prove oneself an expert "puzzle solver" (see Kuhn, 1962, pp. 36–37).

Let $\wp$ be a specified population of individual consumers ν, where $\nu = 1, 2, \ldots, N$. Let $X^{(\nu)}(M^{(\nu)}, p; \alpha)$ be a system of n commodity demand functions ascribed to individual consumer ν. The individual consumer's demand function may satisfy the above three conditions or it may not; it makes no difference. Here $M^{(\nu)}$ is the total money expenditure on commodities by ν in a specified time period; $\bar{M}$ is the per capita total expenditure of $\wp$; p is a vector of n market prices for that time period; and α is a vector of personal and population characteristics. The system of demand functions can be rationalized by a direct utility function $U^{(\nu)}(X; \theta^{(\nu)})$ having the GFT form (2.1) with its vector $\theta^{(\nu)}$ of preference parameters dependent on budget constraint prices p, $M^{(\nu)}$, and α. That is, the system of demand functions $X^{(\nu)}(M^{(\nu)}, p; \alpha)$ can always be derived from the ordinal direct utility function:

$$U^{(\nu)}(X; \theta^{(\nu)}) = \prod_{i=1}^{n} (X_i - \gamma_i)^{\theta_i^{(\nu)}}, \tag{2.33}$$

where:

$$X_i > \max\{0, \gamma_i\}, \tag{2.34}$$

$$\theta = \sum_{i=1}^{n} \theta_i^{(\nu)}(M^{(\nu)}, p; \alpha)$$

for every $\nu = 1, 2, \ldots, N$; here θ, is a positive but otherwise arbitrarily valued function of p, α, and all individual consumers' expenditures. The positive-valued utility function parameters $\theta_i^{(\nu)}(M^{(\nu)}, p; \alpha)$[20] are dependent on the characteristics α, on one or more of the prices p, and on total expenditure, $M^{(\nu)}$, that appear in the consumer's budget constraint

$$\sum_{i=1}^{n} p_i X_i = M^{(\nu)} \tag{2.35}$$

---

[20]Hereafter we shall use $\theta_i^{(\nu)}$ as an abbreviation of $\theta_i^{(\nu)}(M^{(\nu)}, p; \alpha)$.

We define the *aggregate GFT direct utility function*[21] as a weighted geometric mean of the individual consumers' direct utility functions, as follows:

$$U(X;\theta) =_{df} \sum_{\nu=1}^{n} \left[U^{(\nu)}\right]^{\kappa^{(\nu)}} \tag{2.36}$$

where:

$$\kappa^{(\nu)} > 0 \tag{2.37}$$

$$\sum_{\nu=1}^{N} \kappa^{(\nu)} = 1$$

If the weights $\kappa^{(\nu)}$ are made proportional to the individual consumer's positive "supernumerary" expenditure, i.e., where

$$\kappa^{(\nu)} = M^{(\nu)} - \sum_{i=1}^{n} \gamma_i p_i, \tag{2.38}$$

then the equilibrium demands $\bar{X}_i^*$, that is, the magnitudes of demand functions derived from the aggregate direct utility function (2.36-2.37) subject to the arithmetic mean of budget constraints (2.35), are identical with the per capita demands over the population of individual consumers. We assume that all consumers face the same budget constraint prices.

With much gain of simplicity of expression and without loss of essential generality, we present the mathematical derivations only for the case in which each of the arbitrary parameters γ_i is zero. From (2.36-2.37) and (2.39) we obtain

$$U(X;\bar{\theta}) = \prod_{\nu=1}^{N} \prod_{i=1}^{n} X_i^{\sum_{i=1}^{n} \theta_i^{(\nu)}} \tag{2.39}$$

$$= \prod_{i=1}^{n} X_i^{\bar{\theta}_i}, \tag{2.40}$$

---

[21]The authors do not interpret (2.36-2.37) as affording a *community preference field*, although it may serve some function for which community preference fields are intended (*cf.* Gorman, 1963).

where,

$$\bar{\theta}_i = \sum_{\nu=1}^{N} \kappa^{(\nu)} \theta_i^{(\nu)}, \quad i = 1, 2, \ldots, n. \tag{2.41}$$

Let $\bar{M}$ be the arithmetic mean of individual consumers' total expenditures $M^{(\nu)}$, for $\nu = 1, 2, \ldots, N$. Demand functions derived by maximizing (2.40) subject to the per capita budget constraint are, (keep in mind that γ_i was assumed to be 0)

$$\bar{X}_i^* = \frac{\sum_{\nu=1}^{N} \kappa^{(\nu)} \theta_i^{(\nu)}}{\sum_{j=1}^{n} \sum_{\nu=1}^{N} \kappa^{(\nu)} \theta_j^{(\nu)}} p_i^{-1} \left[\bar{M} - \sum_{k=1}^{n} \gamma_k p_k \right] + \gamma_i \tag{2.42}$$

$$= \frac{1}{\theta} \left(\sum_{\nu=1}^{N} \kappa^{(\nu)} \theta_i^{(\nu)} \right) p_i^{-1} \left[\bar{M} - \sum_{k=1}^{n} \gamma_k p_k \right] + \gamma_i \tag{2.43}$$

$$i = 1, 2, \ldots, n.$$

From (2.40) it is apparent that the aggregate direct utility function has the same form in its arguments and parameters as has each individual consumer's GFT direct utility function (2.36); from (2.41) it is readily apparent the per capita demand functions derived from the aggregate direct utility function have the same form in its arguments and parameters as those derived from the individual consumer's direct utility function. Using the relation

$$\frac{\theta_i^{(\nu)}}{\theta} = \frac{p_i X_i^{(\nu)}(M^{(\nu)}, p : \alpha)}{M^{(\nu)}}, \quad i = 1, 2, \ldots, n, \tag{2.44}$$

we get

$$\bar{X}_i^* = \sum_{\nu=1}^{N} \frac{\kappa^{(\nu)} X_i^{(\nu)}(M^{(\nu)}, p; \alpha)}{M^{(\nu)}}, \quad i = 1, 2, \ldots, n. \tag{2.45}$$

In the special case where weights are specified by

$$\kappa^{(\nu)} = \frac{M^{(\nu)}}{\sum_{\nu=1}^{N} M^{(\nu)}}, \quad \nu = 1, 2, \ldots, N, \tag{2.46}$$

we obtain

$$\bar{X}_i^* = \frac{1}{N} \sum_{\nu=1}^{N} X_i^{(\nu)}(M^{(\nu)}, p, \alpha), \quad i = 1, 2, \ldots, n. \tag{2.47}$$

In other words, under specification (2.44) the magnitude of the aggregate demand function (2.41) derived from the *aggregate direct utility function* (2.40) is the arithmetic mean of magnitudes of individual consumer demand functions derived from (2.36).

Chapter 3

Estimating the GFT Form

3.1 Introduction

Empirical tests of the Slutsky property of demand functions tend to dis-
confirm fixed preference utility theory. In particular we refer to the tests
of the Slutsky property by Christensen, Jorgenson and Lau (1975); Barten
and Geyskens (1975); Theil (1975); Berndt, Darrough and Diewert (1977a,
1977b, 1977c); Rosen (1978); Lau, Lin and Totopoulous (1978); Conrad
and Jorgenson (1979a, 1979b) and Deaton and Muellbauer (1980b). By
'fixed preference utility theory' we mean theory based on the assumption that, apart from random disturbances, consumers' preferences are
constant and, in particular, they do not depend on prices p_j paid for commodities or on total expenditure, M, (*i.e.* there is no preference-changing
variable such that (1.4) is not equal to zero). Systems of demand functions derived from fixed preference utility theory always possess the *Slutsky*
property as outlined in Chapter II and depend solely on current prices paid
and total expenditure. If a system of demand functions contains a systematic variable other than prices and total expenditure, or if it does not
possess the Slutsky property, then the underlying direct utility function
cannot be a fixed preference utility function, *cf.* Basmann and Slottje
(1985, 1987).

Possession of the Slutsky property does not imply that the system of
demand functions can be rationalized by a fixed preference utility function, however, *cf.* [Pollak (1977, p. 70) and Basmann, Molina and Slottje
(1983)]. In each of the tests on fixed preference utility theory discussed

above, the selected level of significance (usually $\alpha = 0.05$) is very "risk averse" to Type I Error. The tests tolerate only a very low theoretical probability of incorrectly "rejecting" the Slutsky property when it holds; they accept a very low power of correctly "rejecting" the Slutsky property when it does not hold. This is not a criticism; any choice of level of significance can be validly defended on a variety of grounds. In some context the consequences of "accepting" fixed preference consumer demand theory when it is false may appear very minor in comparison with consequences of "rejecting" fixed preference consumer demand theory when it holds. Still the fact that the 5 percent level of significance used in these tests is so very generous to the null hypotheses tends to diminish the cogency of those tests that are reported to be favorable to the Slutsky property [Barten and Geyskens (1975), Theil (1975), Conrad and Jorgenson (1979a)], and it enhances the cogency of the unfavorable outcomes reported;[Christensen et.al. (1975), Berndt, Darrow and Diewert (1977b-c), Rosen (1978), Conrad and Jorgenson (1979b)][1]

There is another asymmetry that diminishes cogency of empirical tests favoring the Slutsky property regardless of the choice of level of signifi-

---

[1] The authors mentioned in this section used expenditure and price data from various countries and different commodity groups. Christensen, Jorgenson, and Lau (1975) used U.S. data as did Rosen (1978). Blanciforti and Green (1984) also worked with U.S. data. Deaton and Muellbauer(1980b) used British data in their study while Lau, Line, and Totopoulous(1978) did Barten and Geyskens (1975) in their study. Theil (1975) used Dutch data and Barten and Geyskens did part of their study with Dutch data too. Finally, Berndt, Darrough, and Diewert (1977) used Canadian data.

Christensen, Jorgenson, and Lau (1975, p. 380) using the translog functional form, flatly reject homogeneity and symmetry. Berndt, Darrough, and Diewert (1977) examined three functional forms; the translog indirect utility function (TL), the generalized Leontief indirect utility functional form (GL), and the generalized Cobb-Douglas indirect utility functional form (GCD). They reject symmetry for (GCD) and (GL)[Berndt, et.al., 1977, p 663] and reject homogeneity for all three forms[Berndt, et.al., p. 664]. Rosen (1978) used the Stone-Geary utility function and rejected symmetry [p. 5129]. Conrad and Jorgenson (1979) used the translog direct and indirect utility functions and they rejected homogeneity in the indirect form [Conrad et.al., p. 163]. They reject symmetry in the direct functional form [Conrad et.al., p. 164]. Lau, Lin and Totopoulous (1975) used a linear logarithmic expenditure system. They accepted symmetry and homogeneity [Lau, et.al., p. 865]. They also used a .05 level of significance [Lau, et.al., p. 855]. Barten and Geyskens as well as Theil, used a .05 level of significance [see Barten (1977), p.46] for these figures. The study by Barten and Geyskens passed symmetry, negativity, and homogeneity at 0.05 level, while Theil passed only symmetry at 0.05.

cance. Possession of the Slutsky property does not imply that the underlying direct utility function is independent of prices paid or income received; [Pollak (1977), Basmann, Molina and Slottje (1983)].

In this chapter we report some new empirical tests of direct utility functions that rationalize systems of demand functions which have the Slutsky property. Three direct utility functions are tested. One is independent of prices and total expenditure. In the second direct utility function tested here, the parameters depend on prices and total expenditure, but the derived demand functions have the Slutsky property; furthermore, that system of demand functions is also derivable from another direct utility function (to be displayed) whose parameters are not dependent on prices or total expenditure. The third direct utility function to be tested, like the second, has parameters that are dependent on prices and total expenditures, yields demand functions that have the Slutsky property, and which are widely reputed to be derivable from a direct utility function (still unknown to us) whose parameters are independent of prices and total expenditure.

All three systems to be tested as null hypotheses here are known to be consistent with the hypothesis that consumers maximize a direct utility function subject only to the traditional budget constraint. The maintained hypothesis for the tests is presented in Sec. 3.2. The three null hypotheses are presented in Sec. 3.4 along with the outcomes of their tests. The precise maintained hypothesis, against which those three null hypotheses are tested, is that consumers maximize a direct utility function having a generalized Fechner-Thurstone form — see (1.4) — subject only to the ordinary budget constraint. In this chapter we shall not consider any alternative hypotheses that imply that consumers do not maximize a direct utility function at all. This chapter is concerned solely with the question whether those generalized Fechner-Thurstone direct utility functions that are compatible with fixed preferences (in the sense indicated above) are able to compete effectively with the alternatives, price-dependent and expenditure-dependent, in the face of empirical data. The data include 5 general commodity groups:

1. Food,

2. Clothing,

3. Housing,

4. Durables and

5. Medical care.

We have included alcohol, tobacco and food consumed at home and away in the first commodity group. The clothing group includes shoes and other outer-wear. All shelter expenditures including maintenance are included in the housing commodity group. Transportation costs have been aggregated into the durables commodity group. The medical group includes all medical costs as well as entertainment, recreation and education expenditures. The data sources for this study are documented in the data appendix A.

Outcomes of the tests of all three null hypotheses severely discredit the assumption that preferences are independent of prices and total expenditure. That is, if one assumes any one of the three systems of Slutsky demand functions to hold, then (in order to reason consistently) one must accept the deductive consequence that the sample of price, quantity and total expenditure data constitutes an occurrence of an exceedingly improbable event. Fortunately, the maximum likelihood estimation and testing of the selected form of direct utility function does not require the use of Taylor approximations. Nor does it involve the uncertainties of an appeal to large sample distribution theory in evaluating the outcome of the likelihood ratio test; the exact small sample distribution of the likelihood ratio statistic yields exact probabilities of test outcomes in our case. Under any of the three null hypotheses, each to the effect that consumers maximize direct utility functions that are independent of prices and total expenditure, the exact probability of the empirical sample is essentially zero.

Outcomes of our tests of fixed preference consumer demand theory add cogency to negative outcomes of tests reported by Christensen, Jorgenson and Lau (1975), Rosen (1978) and other tests already mentioned. The stringency of the unfavorable outcomes of the tests we report here, indicates a need for a more thorough theoretical and empirical examination of consumer demand functions that can be derived from direct utility functions in which prices, total expenditure and possible other economic magnitudes appear as explicit parameters.

Let $U(X;\theta)$ be a direct utility function with continuous second partial derivatives with respect to X_i, $i = 1,2,\ldots,n$, where θ designates the vector of n adjustable parameters θ_i of $U(X;\theta)$. Let $R_i^{(k)}(X;\theta)$, $i = 1,2,\ldots,n$, $i \neq k$, designate the marginal rate of substitution of X_k for X_i at the point X of the budget domain. Let the adjustable parameters θ_i be real-valued functions $\theta_i(Z)$ of m real-valued magnitudes $Z_1,\ldots,Z_m$. Finally, let the marginal rates of substitution $R_i^{(k)}(X;\theta(Z))$ $\forall\ i,k$ be differentiable with respect to $Z_1,\ldots,Z_m$ at every point X of the budget domain. Let $X^{(0)}$ be any such point, and let $X^{(0)}$ be fixed for the following differentiation of the $R_i^{(k)}(X;\theta(Z))$ with respect to Z_q, $q = 1,2,\ldots,m$. If $\partial R_i^{(k)}/\partial Z_q \neq 0$, then a change in Z_q produced a change in the slopes and curvatures of the indifference surface of $U(X;\theta)$ at $X^{(0)}$. Following Ichimura (1951) and Tintner (1952), we consider Z_q to be a preference-changing variable for $U(X;\theta)$ at $X^{(0)}$ if, and only if, a variation of Z_q produced a change in the slopes and curvatures of the indifference surface $U(X;\theta)$ is constant at $X^{(0)}$.

It is convenient to express effects of a change of arguments of a function on its value in terms of mathematical elasticity, or logarithmic derivatives, and we have continued that practice with respect to the marginal rates of substitution $R_i^{(k)}$ cf. Basmann (1956) and Basmann, Molina and Slottje, (1983)

Finally, primarily as a policy of research economy, we have currently elected to restrict hypothesis testing to the subclass of direct utility functions $U(X;\theta)$ for which elasticities of marginal rates of substitution $R_i^{(k)}(X;\theta)$ are constant over the budget domain (of X). Adoption of this research policy leads directly to the following form of $U(X;\theta)$

$$U(X;\theta) = \prod_{i=1}^{n} X_i^{\theta_i}, \qquad (3.1)$$

$$\theta_i = \beta_i \prod_{k=1}^{n} Z_k^{\sigma_{ik}},$$

$$\beta_i > 0,$$

$$\sum_{i=1}^{n} \beta_k = 1.$$

We refer to (3.2) together with the demand functions derived from it as the constant MRS-elasticity theory of variable consumer preferences. Re-

striction of our current hypothesis testing to this special theory of variable
consumer preferences should not be construed as a claim to know (or even
to believe) that it is in better agreement with reality than alternative
theories of variable preferences.[2]

In this chapter the only potential preference-changing variables to be
considered are prices, p_j, and total expenditure, M. This does not imply
a belief that other preference-changing variables are unimportant.[3] Our
reasons are as follows: As preference-changers, however, prices and total

---

[2]Basmann (1977) has used Department of Commerce data like those in Appendix A
to test fixed preferences against the following alternative specification of parameters θ_i
in the direct utility function

$$\theta_i = a_i + \frac{C_{i,0}}{M} + \frac{C_{i,1}}{M_{t-1}} + u_i \quad i = 1, 2, \ldots, n.$$

where

$$\sum_{i=1}^{n} C_{i,s} = 0 \quad s = 0, 1$$

$$\sum_{i=1}^{n} u_i = 0,$$

and $u = (u_i, \ldots, u_n)$ is a random vector with zero mean vector and finite covariance
matrix. Elasticities of marginal rates of substitution with respect to current and lagged
total expenditure M and M_{t-1} are not constant under this specification. This specification of an elementary variable preference hypothesis fits the eleven commodity grouping
of Department of Commerce data used in (1977) equally closely as the maintained hypothesis H_m described in sec. 3.2 below. In a later study we propose to examine them
as competing hypotheses in the face of the eleven commodity grouping of Department of
Commerce data provided by Blanciforti and Green (1981).

In his doctoral dissertation, Edwin Stecher estimated the expenditure functions derived from (3.1) with the specifications above using the eighty commodity grouping of
Department of Commerce data. (Stecher, 1978, pp. 62-63.)

[3]Basmann (1955, 1956) studied advertisement as a preference changing parameter in
the demand for tobacco. We have done a preliminary study in which the eleven commodities (see Appendix A) have been aggregated into three: (1) durables, (2) nondurables,
and (3) services. The advertising level was constructed by dividing the advertising expenditure on the ith commodity by the overall price level. (Source: U.S. Department of
Commerce) Hence, the maintained hypothesis (3.2) included total expenditure, the price
for each one of the commodities, and z_1 and z_2 are the real expenditures on advertising
by the sellers for durable and nondurable commodities respectively. Our preliminary results indicated that the null hypothesis, that M, p_1, and p_3 have no effect on preferences,
could be rejected at .001 level of significance.

expenditure call for special study, in that they exert two different effects
on derived demand functions one being due to their presence in the utility function parameters and the other effect due to their presence in the
budget constraint, *i.e.*, the substitution effect and the income effect, [Bas-
mann, Molina and Slottje (1983)]. Other preference-changers exert effect
only via parameters of the direct utility function. Another reason for
confining attention to prices and total expenditure as preference-changers
is the special role they play in Veblen's theory of economic growth and
change.

Veblen (1899) put forward an explanatory theory of the utility of commodities that attempts to account for the formation and change of consumer preferences over time.[4] Briefly, utility is a property of the acts of
purchasing, owning or controlling, and consuming commodities. Actually,
the utility of commodities is viewed as a resultant of two kinds of utility, which compete with each other in affecting the consumers' responses
to changes in prices consumers must pay and to the consumer's abilities
to pay, *i.e.*, the total expenditure of which a consumer is capable. Primary utility arises from the direct service of consumption to enhance life
and well-being on the whole (Veblen, 1899, p. 99); the purchase, ownership and consumption of commodities is invested with secondary utility as
evidence or social confirmation of the consumer's relative ability to pay.
Goods are produced and consumed as a means to the fuller unfolding of
human life and their utility consists, in the first instance, in their efficiency
as a means to this end. *But the human proclivity to emulation has seized*
upon the consumption of goods as a means to an invidious comparison, and
has thereby invested consumable goods with a secondary utility as evidence
of relative ability to pay, cf. Veblen, 1899, pp. 154-55. Expenditure that
is motivated chiefly by anticipated secondary utility and which does not
serve human life or well-being in obvious ways Veblen called conspicuous
consumption or "waste", an admittedly unfortunate term (Veblen, 1899,

---

[4]Veblen did not propose a mathematical form for a utility function. His remarks
about utility as a property of the act of purchasing, owning, controlling, and consuming
commodities are open to a variety of reasonable interpretations when it comes to describing substantive utility in the mathematical form of a utility function or index. Veblen's
concepts are transparently consistent with attribution of maximizing behavior to real
consumers (Veblen, 1899, p. 158). Veblen was very critical of the classical school and the
marginal-utility school – Jevons and the Austrians – for their uncritical acceptance of the
hedonistic calculus. (Veblen, 1908, 1909, pp. 181-182; also Veblen, 1909, pp. 232-235)

p. 97), since such expenditure is not recognized as conspicuous consumption or waste in the vulgar sense by the consumer who makes it (Veblen, 1899, p. 99).

In the present connection it must be emphasized that Veblen considered this secondary utility of commodities to be pervasive rather than confined to a few unusual commodities. According to Veblen, consumption goods, and even productive goods, generally possess and exhibit a mixture of primary and secondary utility:

> It would be hazardous to assert that a useful purpose is ever absent from the utility of any article or of any service, however, obviously its prime purpose and chief element is conspicuous waste; and it would be only less hazardous to assert of any primarily useful product that the element of waste is in no way concerned in its value, immediately, or remotely. (Veblen, 1899, p. 101).

Later, in the chapter *"Pecuniary Canons of Taste,"* Veblen suggests that there are no goods supplied in any trade which do not have secondary utility in greater or less degree. (Veblen, 1899, p. 157)

According to Veblen's theory, conspicuous consumption, or the consumption of goods and services that is motivated predominantly by secondary utility, is not confined to the leisure class but prevails over all the social and income classes from richest to poorest. The less affluent classes emulate the consumption patterns and thereby learn and internalize the taste of the more affluent so far as ability to pay will permit. (Veblen, 1899, pp. 83-85, p. 103) Finally, secondary utility is not weak relative to primary utility and has far-reaching consequences for economic growth and change. According to Veblen, next to the instinct for self-preservation *"the propensity for emulation is probably the strongest and most alert of the economic motives proper. ... The need of conspicuous waste, therefore, stands ready to absorb any increase in the community's industrial efficiency or output of goods, after the most elementary physical wants have been provided for."* (Veblen, 1899, pp. 110-111).

This brief review of Veblen's theory of the utility of commodities makes clear the practical motive for assuming that prices and total expenditure have some influence on the parameters of a direct utility function that is supposed to be a mathematical description of the resultant effects of primary and secondary utility in Veblen's sense. Price changes and changes in ability to pay affect consumer demand in two distinct ways:

1. a change in the budget constraint on utility maximization and

2. at each point of the commodity space a change in the marginal rates of substitution between commodities via effect on the relative secondary utilities of commodities.

Furthermore, the review of Veblen's substantive theory of utility helps to make clear why we have specified a direct utility function that is explicit in the form of its dependence on quantities of commodities and explicit in the form of its parameters' dependence on prices and total expenditure. Without such an explicit form of direct utility function confronting the data, we could not separately estimate and test the empirical effects of secondary utility (Veblen effects) of price and total expenditure changes from their ordinary substitution and income effects on consumer demand.

Statistical estimates of utility function parameters are a useful by-product of the conduct of the tests of the fixed preference hypotheses. In Sec. 3.4 we present estimates of the effects of price-changes and total expenditure changes on the parameters of the utility function, and interpret them in terms of Veblen's concepts.

3.2   The Maintained Hypothesis

For this study the maintained hypothesis H_m is the class of all direct utility functions discussed in chapter one,

$$U(X; p, M, u) = \prod_{i=1}^{n} X_i^{\beta_i M^{\sigma_{i0}} \left(\prod_{i=1}^{n} p_j^{\sigma_{ij}} \right) u_i} \tag{3.2}$$

where

$$\beta_i > 0 \tag{3.3}$$

$$\sum_{i=1}^{n} \beta_i = 1.$$

where u is a n-vector of lognormal latent random variables with mean vector $(0, 0, \ldots, 0)$ and finite variance matrix Γ_0. [The remaining stochastic properties attributed to u will be described in the next section.] As we saw in chapter 1, at each point X, the marginal rate of substitution of commodity k for commodity i is the ratio of first partial derivatives of $U(X; p, M, u)$ with respect to X_i and X_n.

$$R_i^{(n)} = \frac{U_i}{U_k} \quad i \neq n \tag{3.4}$$

$$= \frac{X_k}{X_i} \frac{\beta_i}{\beta_n} M^{\omega_{i0}^{(n)}} \prod_{j=1}^{n} p_j^{\omega_{ij}^{(n)}} \frac{u_i}{u_k}$$

where

$$\omega_{i0}^{(n)} = \sigma_{i0} - \sigma_{n0} \tag{3.5}$$

$$\omega_{ij}^{(n)} = \sigma_{ij} - \sigma_{nj}.$$

In keeping with a half-century tradition of consumer demand theory (Hicks and Allen, 1934) we require the direct utility function (3.4) to be ordinal only, and replaceable everywhere in use by any function $\phi(U)$ such that $\phi\prime(U) > 0$ for all points X in question (*cf.* Hicks and Allen, 1934, p.55, p.60; Hicks, 1956, pp. 16-19, 308-309). Obviously, the magnitudes of the logarithmic derivatives σ_{i0} and σ_{ij} (elasticities) of marginal utilities are arbitrary, although the magnitudes of the differences between them are not. (*cf.* Basmann, 1954; 1956, p. 51; Basmann, Molina, and Slottje, 1983). Notice that:

$$\omega_{i0}^{(n)} = \frac{\partial R_i^{(n)}}{\partial M} \frac{M}{R_i^{(n)}}; \tag{3.6}$$

$$\omega_{ij}^{(n)} = \frac{\partial R_i^{(n)}}{\partial p_j} \frac{p_j}{R_i^{(n)}}.$$

The parameters $\omega_{i0}^{(n)}$ and $\omega_{ij}^{(n)}$ are elasticities of the marginal rate of substitution $R_i^{(k)}$ of commodity k for i; $\omega_{i0}^{(k)}$ is the elasticity of $R_i^{(k)}$ with respect to total expenditure M, and $\omega_{ij}^{(k)}$ is the elasticity of $R_i^{(k)}$ with respect to price p_j. We shall refer to the $\omega_{i0}^{(k)}$ as MRS-elasticities with respect to (*wrt*) total expenditure, and to the parameters $\omega_{ij}^{(k)}$ as MRS-elasticities *wrt* to p_j. We shall refer to the parameters $\omega_{ii}^{(k)}$ as own-price MRS-elasticities and to the $\omega_{ij}^{(k)}$ $j \neq k$, as cross-price MRS-elasticities. MRS-elasticities of the marginal rate of substitution $R_i^{(k)}$ with respect to the latent random variables u_i and u_k are $+1$ and -1 respectively. The random variables u_i and u_n are latent random preference changers in this sense for all i, n. Total expenditure, M, is an observable systematic preference-changer if, and only if, $\omega_{i0}^{(k)} \neq 0$ for at least one i, k. A price p_j is an observable systematic preference changer if, and only if, $\omega_{ij}^{(n)} \neq 0$ for some i, n.

From (3.4) it is apparent that, although the total number of $\omega_{i0}^{(n)}$ is n^2, there are only $(n-1)$ independent MRS-elasticities *wrt* to total expenditure, M. Notice (for later reference in this section) that H_m implies the restrictions

$$\sum_{i=1}^{n-1} \omega_{i0}^{(i+1)} + \omega_{n0}^{(1)} = 0 \quad i = 1, 2, \ldots, n \tag{3.7}$$

$$\omega_{k0}^{(k)} = 0,$$

Furthermore, there are n^3 MRS-elasticities $\omega_{ij}^{(k)}$ *wrt* prices. However, there are only $(n+1)(n-1)$ independent elasticities $\omega_{ij}^{(k)}$. Notice that H_m deductively implies the following restrictions:

$$\sum_{i=1}^{n-1} \omega_{ij}^{(i+1)} + \omega_{nj}^{(1)} = 0 \quad j = 1, 2, \ldots, n \tag{3.8}$$

$$\omega_{kj}^{(k)} = 0, \quad \forall j, k$$

The restrictions (3.7) and (3.8) implied by the direct utility function (3.2) will be imposed on the maximum likelihood estimators under H_m and the null hypotheses to be described at the beginning of Sec. 3.4. This is done for two closely related practical reasons:

1. Imposition of those restrictions on maximum likelihood estimators under H_m ensures that tests of the null hypotheses that imply or are consistent with fixed preference utility theory are fair to the latter.

2. Impositions of those restrictions on the maximum likelihood estimators enables us to use a *minimally sufficient statistic* for the parameters of (3.2), *i.e.*, to ensure that the parameter estimates incorporate

all relevant empirical information that is available in the expenditure data. (Graybill, 1976, pp. 69-71, 75-76)

Some additional restrictions on the MRS-elasticities are mentioned now for later reference in this and subsequent sections:

$$\omega_{k0}^{(i)} = -\omega_{i0}^{(k)} \ \forall \ i,k \tag{3.9}$$

$$\omega_{i0}^{(k)} = \omega_{i0}^{(j)} - \omega_{k0}^{(j)}$$

$$\omega_{ij}^{(k)} = \omega_{ij}^{(m)} - \omega_{kj}^{(m)} \ \forall \ i,j,k \tag{3.10}$$

$$\omega_{ij}^{(k)} = \omega_{jj}^{(k)} - \omega_{jj}^{(i)}$$

$$\omega_{kj}^{(i)} = -\omega_{ij}^{(k)}$$

Restrictions (3.9) and (3.10) will be found useful chiefly in facilitating the discussion of statistical estimates of MRS-elasticities in Sec. 3.4 in the light of Veblen's theory.

Demand functions are derived by maximizing the direct utility function (3.2) with respect to X_i subject to the ordinary budget constraint

$$\sum_{i=1}^{n} p_i X_i = M. \tag{3.11}$$

The demand functions are

$$X_i^* = \frac{\frac{\beta_i}{\beta_n} M^{\sigma_{i0}^{(n)}} \left(\prod_{j=1}^{n} p_j^{\sigma_{ij}^{(n)}} \right) \frac{u_i}{u_n}}{K(p,M)} \frac{M}{p_i} \tag{3.12}$$

where

$$K(p,M) = \sum_{h=1}^{n-1} \frac{\beta_i}{\beta_n} M^{\sigma_{i0}^{(n)}} \left(\prod_{j=1}^{n} p_j^{\sigma_{ij}^{(n)}} \right) \frac{u_i}{u_n} + 1$$

In general the demand functions (3.12) do not possess the Slutsky property.

The equations used to confront the price and expenditure data directly in the *general linear hypothesis* form are expressions for logarithms of the commodity expenditure ratios M_i/M_k where $M_i = pX_i^*$, $i,k = 1,2,\ldots,n$, $k \neq i$, derived from (3.2) or equivalently (3.12):

$$\ln \frac{M_i}{M_n} = \ln \frac{\beta_i}{\beta_n} + \omega_{i0}^{(n)} \ln M + \sum_{j=1}^{n} \omega_{ij}^{(n)} \ln p_j + \eta_i^{(n)} \qquad (3.13)$$

where the random variable $\eta_i^{(n)}$ is defined by

$$\eta_i^{(n)} = \ln u_i - \ln u_n.$$

Under the maintained hypothesis H_m it follows that the random disturbances in (3.13) are normally distributed with zero means and finite variances and covariances. The remaining stochastic properties H_m attributes to the $\eta_i^{(n)}$ will be described at the end of this section. Since each of the expressions (3.13) is linear in its unknown intercept and unknown coefficient of $\ln M$ and $\ln p_j$, it is more efficient to use (3.13) to confront the empirical data directly than to use (say) Taylor expansions of expressions for budget shares M_i/M or their logarithms.

Although there are $n(n-1)$ behavioral relations (3.13) they are not independent. The rank of the whole system is $(n-1)$. However, a suitably chosen subsystem containing n-behavioral equations, having rank $(n-1)$, can serve as a basis for the remaining equations. For instance, select a system, S, of n-behavioral equations from (3.13) as follows: Let $k = i+1$ for $i = 1,2,\ldots,n-1$ and let $k = 1$ for $i = n$. Since

$$\sum_{i=1}^{n-1} \ln \frac{M_i}{M_{i+1}} + \ln \frac{M_n}{M_1} = 0, \qquad (3.14)$$

$$\sum_{i=1}^{n-1} \eta_i^{(i+1)} + \eta_n^{(1)} = 0$$

it follows from (3.7) and (3.8) that the rank of the n equations is $(n-1)$. Furthermore, from the MRS-elasticities $\omega_{i0}^{(i+1)}$ $i = 1,2,\ldots,n-1$, and $\omega_{n0}^{(1)}$ appearing in the system S, the remaining $(n^2 - 1)\omega_{i0}^{(k)}$ in (3.7) can be determined by means of equations (3.9). In like manner from the MRS-elasticities $\omega_{ij}^{(i+1)}$ $i = 1,2,\ldots,n-1$, $\omega_{nj}^{(1)}$, $j = 1,2,\ldots,n$ in the system S the remaining $\omega_{ij}^{(n)}$ can be determined by means of equations (3.10). Finally, from the n intercepts in the system S, the parameters $\beta_1,\ldots,\beta_n$ can be determined from equation (3.13).

Consider the latent random preference changers $\eta_i^{(i+1)}$, $i = 1, 2, \ldots, n-1$, appearing in the system S. Let $(\Lambda_0^{(S)}, \Lambda_1^{(S)}, \ldots, \Lambda_\nu^{(S)}, \ldots,)$ represent successive serial covariance matrices of those random preference-changers. $\Lambda_\nu^{(S)}$ $\nu = 0, 1, 2, \ldots$ is $(n \times n)$ but of rank $(n-1)$; cf. (3.14). For every $\nu = 0, 1, 2, \ldots$ the serial covariance matrix Λ_ν of all latent random preference-changers appearing in (3.13) is determined by (3.13) and $\Lambda_\nu^{(S)}$. Let any hypothetical serial covariance scheme $(\Lambda_0^{(S)}, \Lambda_1^{(S)}, \ldots, \Lambda_\nu^{(S)}, \ldots)$ be specified. As a consequence of (3.14) the ordinary Gauss-Aitken estimators (Aitken, 1935; Wold, 1953, pp. 208-209) of the intercepts and MRS-elasticities $\omega_{i0}^{(n)}, \omega_{ij}^{(n)}$ appearing in (3.13) satisfy all of the theoretical restrictions (3.7) - (3.10) on $\beta_1, \ldots, \beta_n$ and MRS-elasticities with respect to total expenditure M and price p_j that are implied by the direct utility function (3.2). Consequently, generalized least squares estimation techniques were used in this study, we will say more on this below.

In concluding this description of the maintained hypothesis we turn to the latent random preference-changers u_i appearing in the direct utility function (3.2), and — consequently — in marginal rates of substitution (3.4), in the demand function (3.12), and the behavioral equations (3.13). Since it is only in the form of logarithms $\eta_i^{(n)}$ of ratios u_i/u_k that the latent random variables enter our estimators and test statistics, we describe the stochastic aspects of the maintained hypothesis H_m in terms of the $\eta_i^{(n)}$, $i, k = 1, 2, \ldots, n$; $k \neq i$.

Rationale for the hypothesis that the non-observable random preference changers are normally distributed is the classical Laplacean rationale: We consider $\eta_i^{(n)}$ to be the sum of many different latent elementary preference-changers each of which is smaller in absolute value than a fixed number L that is in turn very small relative to the standard deviation of their sum; from these assumptions it follows that the $\eta_i^{(n)}$ will be approximately normally distributed. The criticisms are the traditional ones, too, being chiefly that no one knows that the number of elementary latent preference changers is sufficiently large for the normal approximation to be accurate enough for the application at hand, etc., cf. Uspensky, 1937, pp. 296-297.

The significance tests reported in Sec. 3.4 are based on the maintained hypothesis that the latent random preference-changers $\eta_i^{(n)}$ are serially correlated over time. In other words, the maintained hypothesis, H_m and each of the null hypotheses to be tested, incorporates the hypothesis that all serial covariance matrices are not null, *i.e.*, that $\Lambda_\nu^{(S)} \neq 0$ for every basis system S for (3.13) and for every $\nu \geq 1$. Of course, by specifying some definite alternative serial covariance matrices then (it is to be expected) the test statistics based on the alternative specification would be numerically different from, and significant at different Type I error probabilities from those if $\Lambda_\nu^{(S)} = 0$. A sensitivity analysis was performed and first order autocorrelation was adjusted for (Basmann (1985)).

The Fisherian reference class for all tests of significance used in this chapter is the hypothetical infinite population of random samples (Fisher, 1922, pp. 311-312; Fisher, 1956, p. 33, p. 77) of commodity group expenditures $M_1, \ldots, M_5$, total expenditure M and commodity group prices $p_1, \ldots, p_5$ being fixed and identical with those described in Appendix A. Consequently, the latent random preference-changers, $\eta_i^{(n)}$ $i = 1, 2, \ldots, 5$, $n \neq i$ are distributed independently of logarithms of total expenditure, M, and prices, p_j, in the behavioral equations (3.13).

3.3 Econometric Specification

3.3.1 Serial Correlation Hypothesis

The theory underlying the specification of the serial correlation hypothesis on the stochastic taste changers $\eta_i^{(\kappa)}$, is given by Basmann (1985).

The theory of serial correlation of the stochastic taste-changers u_{ti} in the utility function (3.2) rests on two chief assumptions, Basmann (1985, p. 199).

Assumption 1 *If every stochastic taste-changer u_{ti} increases or decreases by the same increment in period t, then each of the marginal rates of substitution $R_i^{(k)}$ $i, k = 1, \ldots, n$, remains invariant (at every point of the domain of $\mathbf{X}$ for all subsequent periods, $t + 1, t + 2, \ldots$).*

Assumption 2 *If there is a ceteris paribus increase in the stochastic taste changer u_{tk}, then*

1. *all of the marginal rates of substitution of k for i, $i \neq k$ change in equal proportion.*

2. *all other marginal rates of substitution $R_i^{(j)}$, where $i \neq k$, $j \neq k$, $i,j = 1, \dots, n$, remains invariant (at every point of the domain of $\mathbf{X}$ for all subsequent periods, $t+1, t+2, \dots$).*

Notice that **Assumption 1** and **Assumption 2** necessarily hold for period t, Basmann (1985, p. 198).

This theory of serial correlation of stochastic taste changers is not limited in application to GFT direct utility functions. In the present application, the **Assumptions 1** and **2** imply that all of the stochastic disturbances $\eta_i^{(k)}$ share the same serial correlogram or — equivalent — spectral density function.

Notice that **Assumptions 1** and **2** are part of the maintained hypothesis here. Consequently they are not tested empirically in this chapter.

Each of the random elements $\eta_i^{(\kappa)}$ given in the previous equations (which were set up to test serial correlation hypotheses) satisfies:

$$\eta_{i,t+2}^{(\kappa)} - \phi_{i,1}\eta_{i,t+1}^{(\kappa)} + \phi_{i,2}\eta_{i,t}^{(\kappa)} = \epsilon_{i,t+2} \quad \forall \, i, \kappa. \tag{3.15}$$

where $E[\epsilon_t] = 0$, $E[\epsilon_t\epsilon_s] = 0$ for $t \neq s$, and $E[\epsilon_t^2] = \sigma_\epsilon^2$. To guarantee a stationary process the roots of the polynomial should lie within the unit-circle of the complex plane which is assured if the Routhian conditions for stability are satisfied. A simple check is made by applying the forward operator $\mathcal{E}$ to (3.15) above which yields the associated homogenous equation:

$$\mathcal{E}^2 - \phi_{i,1}\mathcal{E} + \phi_{i,2} = 0 \tag{3.16}$$

which implies the following Routhian conditions:[5]

$$1 - \phi_{i,1} + \phi_{i,2} > 0 \tag{3.17}$$

$$1 + \phi_{i,1} + \phi_{i,2} > 0 \tag{3.18}$$

$$1 - \phi_{i,2} > 0 \tag{3.19}$$

The elements of the autocovariance matrix:

$$E\left[\eta_i^{(\kappa)}\eta_i^{\kappa\prime}\right] = Z = \sigma_{\epsilon_i}^2 \Phi \tag{3.20}$$

---

[5]see Kenkle (1974) for an excellent discussion on the conditions for stability

are easily derived from the variance:

$$\sigma_{\eta_i}^2 = \frac{(1 + \phi_{i,2})\,\sigma_{\epsilon_i}^2}{(1 - \phi_{i,2})\left[(1 + \phi_{i,2})^2 - \phi_{i,1}^2\right]} \tag{3.21}$$

and the autocorrelation coefficients:

$$\rho_{i,1} = \frac{\phi_{i,1}}{1 + \phi_{i,2}} \tag{3.22}$$

$$\rho_{i,2} = \frac{\phi_{i,1}^2}{1 + \phi_{i,2}} - \phi_{i,2} \tag{3.23}$$

and

$$\rho_{i,s} = \phi_{i,1}\rho_{i,s-1} - \phi_{i,2}\rho_{i,s-2}, \quad s > 2 \tag{3.24}$$

The inverse of Φ_i, (Φ_i^{-1}) is given by:

$$\begin{pmatrix}
1 & -\phi_{i,1} & \phi_{i,2} & 0 & \cdots & 0 & 0 \\
-\phi_{i,1} & 1 + \phi_{i,1}^2 & -\phi_{i,1} - \phi_{i,1}\phi_{i,2} & \phi_{i,2} & \cdots & 0 & 0 \\
\phi_{i,2} & -\phi_{i,1} - \phi_{i,1}\phi_{i,2} & 1 + \phi_{i,1}^2 + \phi_{i,2}^2 & -\phi_{i,1} - \phi_{i,1}\phi_{i,2} & \cdots & 0 & 0 \\
0 & \phi_{i,2} & -\phi_{i,1} - \phi_{i,1}\phi_{i,2} & 1 + \phi_{i,1}^2 + \phi_{i,2}^2 & \cdots & 0 & 0 \\
\vdots & \vdots & \vdots & \vdots & \ddots & \vdots & \vdots \\
0 & 0 & 0 & 0 & \cdots & 1 + \phi_{i,1}^2 & -\phi_{i,1} \\
0 & 0 & 0 & 0 & \cdots & -\phi_{i,1} & 1
\end{pmatrix} \tag{3.25}$$

From (3.25) above a matrix Λ_i can be formed such that $\Lambda_i'\Lambda_i = \Phi_i^{-1}$ which is given by:

$$\Lambda_i = \begin{pmatrix}
\sigma_\epsilon/\sigma_\eta & 0 & 0 & 0 & \cdots & 0 & 0 \\
-\rho_1\sqrt{1 - \phi_{i,2}^2} & \sqrt{1 - \phi_{i,2}^2} & 0 & 0 & \cdots & 0 & 0 \\
\phi_{i,2} & -\phi_{i,1} & 1 & 0 & \cdots & 0 & 0 \\
0 & \phi_{i,2} & -\phi_{i,1} & 1 & \cdots & 0 & 0 \\
\vdots & \vdots & \vdots & \vdots & \ddots & \vdots & \vdots \\
0 & 0 & 0 & 0 & \cdots & 1 & 0 \\
0 & 0 & 0 & 0 & \cdots & -\phi_{i,1} & 1
\end{pmatrix} \tag{3.26}$$

where:

$$\sigma_{\epsilon_i}/\sigma_{\eta_i} = \sqrt{\frac{(1 - \phi_{i,2})\left[(1 + \phi_{i,2})^2 - \phi_{i,1}^2\right]}{1 + \phi_{i,2}}} \tag{3.27}$$

As seen in (3.26) above $\rho_{i,1}$ is given in terms of $\phi_{i,1}$ and $\phi_{i,2}$. Consequently if $\phi_{i,1}$ and $\phi_{i,2}$ are known the Generalized Least Squares (GLS) estimators are given by:

$$\hat{\beta}_i = \left(x_i' \Phi_i^{-1} x_i \right)^{-1} x_i' \Phi_i^{-1} y_i \tag{3.28}$$

Since the models used above assume $x_i = x_j$ for $i, j = 1, 2, \ldots, n$ 3.28 may be obtained by applying the transformation Λ_i to the original data and utilizing Ordinary Least Squares (OLS) to obtain efficient estimators. For some restricted models[6], the Seemingly Unrelated Regressions (SUR) estimation procedure[7] is employed to obtain efficient parameter estimates for the system.[8]

3.3.2 Likelihood Support for Hypotheses

Since a multiple equation system is used likelihood support for various hypothesis is assessed by finding and analyzing a system variance covariance matrix in order to facilitate the following. Let:

$$Y_i = \Lambda_i y_i \tag{3.29}$$

$$\mathbf{Y} = (\, Y_1, \quad Y_2, \quad \ldots, \quad Y_n \,) \tag{3.30}$$

$$X = \Lambda_i x_i = \Lambda_j x_j \quad i, j = 1, 2, \ldots, n \tag{3.31}$$

$$\mathbf{B} = (\, \beta_1, \quad \beta_2, \quad \ldots, \quad \beta_n \,) \tag{3.32}$$

$$u = \mathbf{Y} - X\mathbf{B} = (\, \epsilon_1, \quad \epsilon_2, \quad \ldots, \quad \epsilon_n, \,) \tag{3.33}$$

$$\hat{\Sigma} = \frac{1}{k} u'u \tag{3.34}$$

Making the additional assumption that $\epsilon_{i,j} \sim N(0, \sigma_{\epsilon_i}^2)$, their joint density function is easily determined, and from their density function we

---

[6]Specifically those involving cross equation restrictions and some zero restrictions.

[7]See Zellner (1962).

[8]In this book it has been assumed that $\phi_{i,1}$ and $\phi_{i,2}$ were the same for each equation in the system refer to the results section for further discussion on this point.

can determine the density function of the observed values of the y's[9] which is the likelihood function we need.[10] Therefore:

$$f(Y_{i,1}, Y_{i,2}, \ldots, Y_{i,k}) = \left| \frac{\partial \epsilon_i}{\partial Y_i} \right| f(\epsilon_{i,1}, \epsilon_{i,2}, \ldots, \epsilon_{i,k}), \quad (3.35)$$

where $|\partial \epsilon_i / \partial Y_i|$ is the absolute value of the determinant:

$$\left| \partial \epsilon_i / \partial Y_i \right| = \begin{vmatrix} \partial \epsilon_{i,1}/\partial Y_{i,1} & \partial \epsilon_{i,1}/\partial Y_{i,2} & \cdots & \partial \epsilon_{i,1}/\partial Y_{i,k} \\ \partial \epsilon_{i,2}/\partial Y_{i,1} & \partial \epsilon_{i,2}/\partial Y_{i,2} & \cdots & \partial \epsilon_{i,2}/\partial Y_{i,k} \\ \vdots & \vdots & \ddots & \vdots \\ \partial \epsilon_{i,k}/\partial Y_{i,1} & \partial \epsilon_{i,k}/\partial Y_{i,2} & \cdots & \partial \epsilon_{i,k}/\partial Y_{i,k} \end{vmatrix} \quad i = 1, 2, \ldots, k$$

$$(3.36)$$

which is the *Jacobian* of the transformation from $u_{i,1}, u_{i,2}, \ldots, u_{i,k}$ to $Y_{i,1}, Y_{i,2}, \ldots, Y_{i,k}$. Using Φ^{-1} above, it can be shown:

$$\begin{aligned} \epsilon_{i,1} &= (\sigma_{\epsilon_i}/\sigma_{\eta_i}) Y_{i,1} - \beta (\sigma_{\epsilon_i}/\sigma_{\eta_i}) X_1 & (3.37) \\ \epsilon_{i,2} &= \left(\sqrt{1 - \phi_{i,2}} Y_{i,2} - \rho_{i,1} \sqrt{1 - \phi_{i,2}} Y_{i,1} \right) \\ & \quad - \beta \left(\sqrt{1 - \phi_{i,2}} X_2 - \rho_{i,1} \sqrt{1 - \phi_{i,2}} X_1 \right) \\ \epsilon_{i,3} &= (Y_{i,3} - \phi_{i,1} Y_{i,2} + \phi_{i,2} Y_{i,1}) - \beta (X_3 - \phi_{i,1} X_2 + \phi_{i,2} X_1) \\ & \vdots \\ \epsilon_{i,k} &= (Y_{i,k} - \phi_{i,1} Y_{i,k-1} + \phi_{i,2} Y_{i,k-2}) - \beta (X_k - \phi_{i,1} X_{k-1} + \phi_{i,2} X_{k-2}) \end{aligned}$$

it is assumed that:

$$\begin{aligned} \phi_{i,1} &= \phi_{j,1} = \phi_1 \\ \phi_{i,2} &= \phi_{j,2} = \phi_2 \end{aligned} \quad (3.38)$$

from (3.37)-(3.39) it follows that

$$\frac{\partial \epsilon_{i,1}}{\partial Y_{i,1}} = (\sigma_{\epsilon_i}/\sigma_{\eta_i}) \quad (3.39)$$

$$\frac{\partial \epsilon_{i,2}}{\partial Y_{i,2}} = \sqrt{1 - \phi_2^2} \quad (3.40)$$

---

[9]See Theorem 11 p. 200 Mood, Graybill, and Boes (1974).

[10]This discussion parallels Judge *et al.* (1985) and Kmenta (1986) but extends it to the multivariate case

$$\frac{\partial \epsilon_{i,t}}{\partial Y_{i,t}} = 1 \qquad t = 3, 4, \ldots, k$$

$$\frac{\partial \epsilon_{i,t}}{\partial Y_{i,s}} = 0 \qquad t \neq s$$

$$\frac{\partial \epsilon_{i,t}}{\partial Y_{j,t}} = 0 \qquad i \neq j \quad i = 1, 2, \ldots, n \qquad (3.41)$$

Therefore $|\partial \epsilon_i / \partial Y_i|$ can be written as

$$|\partial \epsilon_i / \partial Y_i| = |\partial \epsilon_j / \partial Y_j| = \begin{vmatrix} \sigma_\epsilon / \sigma_\eta & 0 & 0 & \cdots & 0 \\ 0 & \sqrt{1 - \phi_2^2} & 0 & \cdots & 0 \\ 0 & 0 & 1 & \cdots & 0 \\ \vdots & \vdots & \vdots & \ddots & \vdots \\ 0 & 0 & 0 & \cdots & 1 \end{vmatrix} \qquad (3.42)$$

Rewriting

$$|\partial \epsilon_i / \partial Y_i| = \sqrt{\left[(1 - \phi_2)^2 \left[(1 + \phi_2)^2 - \phi_1^2 \right] \right]} \quad i = 1, 2, \ldots, n \qquad (3.43)$$

The log likelihood function for the system is given by:[11]

$$L = \frac{1}{2} \ln \left| \frac{\partial \mathbf{u}}{\partial \mathbf{y}} \right|^2 - \frac{T}{2} \ln \left| \hat{\Sigma} \right| \qquad (3.44)$$

where:

$$\left| \frac{\partial \mathbf{u}}{\partial \mathbf{y}} \right| = \begin{vmatrix} \left(\frac{\partial \epsilon_1}{\partial Y_1} \right) & 0 & \cdots & 0 \\ 0 & \left(\frac{\partial \epsilon_2}{\partial Y_2} \right) & \cdots & 0 \\ \vdots & \vdots & \ddots & \vdots \\ 0 & 0 & \cdots & \left(\frac{\partial \epsilon_n}{\partial Y_n} \right) \end{vmatrix} \qquad (3.45)$$

From (3.42) and (3.45)

$$\left| \frac{\partial \mathbf{u}}{\partial \mathbf{y}} \right|^2 = \left[(1 - \phi_2)^2 \left[(1 + \phi_2)^2 - \phi_1^2 \right] \right]^n \qquad (3.46)$$

A grid search method is employed in this book where fifty pairs of autocorrelation parameters ϕ_1 and ϕ_2 are selected and the data, which is setup to conform with each model, is transformed using equation (3.26) above. Likelihood support is then assessed for each of the alternative pairs by comparison of their respective generalized variances.

---

[11]Constant terms have been left off for notational simplicity.

3.4   Tests of Fixed Preference Hypotheses

Within the class H_m of direct utility functions (3.2) there is one obvious subclass $H_0^{(1)}$ (to be described) for which preferences are independent of prices and total expenditure. However, there is another subclass $H_0^{(2)}$ (to be described) of direct utility functions (3.2) that generate consumer demand functions (3.12) which are also derivable from a known explicit fixed preference direct utility function to be given presently. Finally, there is a third subclass $H_0^{(3)}$ (to be described) of direct utility functions (3.2) that generate consumer demand functions that are widely considered to be derivable from a (as yet unknown) fixed preference direct utility function. We shall refer to $H_0^{(2)}$ and $H_0^{(3)}$ as classes of fixed-preference compatible direct utility functions. In this section we show that the expenditure and price data discredit these three hypothetical fixed-preference compatible direct utility functions.

The most restrictive null hypothesis we have tested is specified by the following restrictions on MRS-elasticities:

$$\omega_{i0}^{(k)} = 0, \quad \forall \; i, k, \; i \neq k \tag{3.47}$$
$$\omega_{ij}^{(k)} = 0, \quad \forall \; i, j, k, \; i \neq k.$$

We call this null hypothesis $H_0^{(1)}$. $H_0^{(1)}$ implies that the direct utility function (3.2) is a weighted geometric mean of quantities X_i, $i = 1, 2, \ldots, n$, *i.e.*,

$$U(X; u) = \prod_{i=1}^{n} X_i^{\beta_i u_i} \tag{3.48}$$

Apart from the presence of the latent random preference-changers u_i, (3.48) is the form first proposed for indifference maps by Thurstone (1931, p.142, p. 147), now called the Cobb-Douglas utility function [Deaton and Muellbauer (1980 , pp. 103, 201, 253)] after Cobb and Douglas (1928) who used the weighted geometric average form for production functions. It is also called the Stone-Geary utility function [e.g. Layard and Walters (1978, pp. 162-163)] after Geary and Stone (see Stone (1954)).

$H_0^{(1)}$ is the only null hypothesis in H_m that unambiguously implies that consumer preferences are independent of prices and total expenditure. $H_0^{(1)}$ implies that variations in preferences, *i.e.*, changes in marginal

TABLE 3.1 Likelihood Ratio Test of Fixed Preference Utility Functions Against Price/Expenditure Dependent Utility Function			
$\dfrac{M_i}{M_k}$ (i,k)	$H_0^{(1)}$ $\omega_{ij}^{(k)} = 0 \ \forall \ i,j$ $\omega_{i0}^{(k)} = 0$	$H_0^{(2)}$ $\omega_{i0}^* = 0$ $\omega_{ij} = 0$	$H_0^{(3)}$ $\omega_{ii}^{(n)} = 1 - \sigma_{i0} \ i \neq k$ $\omega_{ik}^{(k)} = -(1-\sigma_{k0}) \ i \neq k$ $\omega_{ij}^{(k)} = 0 \ \ j \neq k$
1,2	8.6782	9.4428	8.1431 (.0021)
2,3	58.8835	27.2399	23.773
3,4	16.5029	14.0803	21.1831
4,5	22.4645	14.9826	17.1362
5,1	173.8342	20.4247	7.9462 (.0002)

rates of transformation (3.4) are caused solely by variations in the non-observable random preference changers u_i, $i = 1, 2, \ldots, n$. The demand functions (3.12) under $H_0^{(1)}$ have the *Klein-Rubin* form (Klein and Rubin, 1947) and possess the Slutsky property. The behavioral relations (3.13) take the simple form:

$$\ln \frac{M_i}{M_k} = \ln \frac{\beta_i}{\beta_k} + \eta_i^{(k)} \quad i = 1, 2, \ldots, n \text{ and } i \neq k. \tag{3.49}$$

Refer to Table 3.1, col. 1. Null hypothesis $H_0^{(1)}$[12] implies that each of the maximum likelihood statistics whose sample values $\hat{F}_i$ are shown in col. 1, is distributed as a central F variate with 6 and 28 degrees of freedom. The number in parentheses shows the maximum probability ("predicted" by $H_0^{(1)}$) with which the test statistic r_1^2 exceeds the number shown in col. 1.[13] Each of the $\hat{F}_i$ in Table 3.1 is extremely improbable under the hypothesis $H_0^{(1)}$ namely, that changes in prices p_j and total expenditure M

---

[12]We emphasize again that only $H_0^{(1)}$ unambiguously implies that consumer preferences are independent of prices and total expenditure.

[13]If no number appears in parenthesis this implies the probability is .0001 or smaller.

do not affect consumer preferences via the marginal rates of substitution (3.4).

Null hypothesis $H_0^{(2)}$ is characterized by the following restrictions:

$$\omega_{ij}^{(k)} = 0 \quad j \neq i, \ i \neq k \tag{3.50}$$

$$\omega_{ii}^{(k)} = \omega \quad \forall \ i \neq k.$$

Under $H_0^{(2)}$ the price-dependent utility function (3.2) becomes

$$U(X;p) = \prod_{i=1}^{n} X_i^{\beta_i p_i^{\omega} u_i} \tag{3.51}$$

Marginal rates of transformation $R_i^{(k)}$ are affected systematically only by the relative price ratio (p_i/p_k); moreover the proportionate effect of a change in p_i/p_k on $R_i^{(n)}$ is the same for all i. Under $H_0^{(2)}$ demand functions (3.12) become

$$X_i = \frac{\beta_i p_i^{\omega} u_i}{\sum_{k=1}^{n} \beta_k p_k^{\omega} u_k} \frac{M}{p_i} \quad i = 1, 2, ..., n. \tag{3.52}$$

The demand functions (3.52) possess the Slutsky property (Basmann, 1968, pp. 159-163).

The chief reason for testing null hypothesis $H_0^{(2)}$ arises from the fact that the demand functions (3.52) are also deducible from the following *fixed preference direct utility function*

$$V(X) = \sum_{i=1}^{n} (\beta_i u_i)^{\frac{1}{1-\omega}} X_i^{\frac{\omega}{\omega-1} - \frac{1}{\omega}}. \tag{3.53}$$

cf. Basmann, Molina and Slottje (1983). Apart from the presence of one non-observable random preference-changer u_i , the utility function $V(X)$ is Bergson's (Bergson, 1936; Sato, 1972, p. 109). The direct utility functions (3.51) and (3.53) are feasibly testable against each other in an incentive-compatible barter experiment (Basmann, Molina and Slottje, 1983). Prices and total expenditures of the experimental subject must be held constant, of course.

Under $H_0^{(2)}$ the behavior relations (3.13) take the form

$$\ln \frac{M_i}{M_k} = \ln \frac{\beta_i}{\beta_k} + \omega_{ii}^{(k)} \ln p_i + \eta_i^{(k)} \tag{3.54}$$

$$\omega_{ii}^{(k)} = \omega \quad i \neq k$$

Refer to Table 3.1 col. 2. $H_0^{(2)}$ implies that the maximum likelihood test statistics whose sample values $\hat{F}_i$ are shown in col. 2 are distributed as a central F variate with 5 and 28 degrees of freedom. For each i, the probability that a central $F_{5,28}$ exceeds the number $\hat{F}_i$ shown in col.2 is smaller than one in ten thousand (0.0001); in many instances, much smaller. Consequently, if preferences are independent of prices and expenditure in accordance with the direct utility function (3.53) or depend on prices p_i in accordance with (3.51), then each of the values of the test statistics shown in col. 2 describes the occurrence of an extremely improbable event.

Null hypothesis $H_0^{(3)}$ is specified by the following restrictions on (3.2):

$$\sigma_{ij} = 0 \quad j \neq i \tag{3.55}$$
$$\sigma_{ii} + \sigma_{i0} = 1 \quad i = 1, 2, \ldots, n$$

Under $H_0^{(3)}$ the direct utility function (3.2) becomes

$$U(X; p, M) = \prod_{i=1}^{n} X_i^{\beta_i M^{\sigma_{i0}} p_i^{1-\sigma_{i0}}} \quad k \neq i \tag{3.56}$$

(See Basmann, Molina and Slottje, 1983). $H_0^{(3)}$ implies that the demand functions have the additive logarithmic form (Leser, 1941; Houthakker, 1960, p. 253; Arrow, 1961; Seo, 1973, pp. 26-32).

$$X_i^* = \frac{\beta_i M^{\sigma_{i0}} p_i^{1-\sigma_{i0}}}{\prod_{k=1}^{n} \beta_k M^{\sigma_{k0}} p_k^{1-\sigma_{k0}}} \frac{M}{p_i} \quad i = 1, 2, \ldots, n. \tag{3.57}$$

The demand functions (3.57) possess the Slutsky property, but existence of a displayable explicit direct utility function $V(X)$ that is independent of prices and total expenditure and from which (3.57) can be derived is problematical (Houthakker, 1960, p. 252n; 1965, p. 801). $H_0^{(3)}$ implies the following restrictions on MRS-elasticities

$$\omega_{ii}^{(k)} = 1 - \sigma_{i0}, \quad i \neq k$$
$$\omega_{ik}^{(k)} = -(1 - \sigma_{k0}), \quad i \neq k$$
$$\omega_{ij}^{(k)} = 0, \quad j \neq k \tag{3.58}$$

From (3.58) it follows that

$$\omega_{i0}^{(k)} + \omega_{ii}^{(k)} + \omega_{ik}^{(k)} = 0 \tag{3.59}$$

Consequently under $H_0^{(3)}$ the behavioral equations (3.13) take the form

$$\ln \frac{M_i}{M_k} = \ln \frac{\beta_i}{\beta_k} + \omega_{i0}^{(k)} \ln M + \omega_{ii}^{(n)} \ln p_i + \omega_{ik}^{(k)} \ln p_k + \eta_i^{(k)} \quad i \neq k. \quad (3.60)$$

$H_0^{(3)}$ implies that (3.60) is homogeneous of degree zero in M, p_i and p_k.

Refer to Table 3.1, col. 3. $H_0^{(3)}$ implies that the maximum likelihood statistics whose sample values $\hat{F}_i$ are shown in col. 3 are distributed as a central F variate with 3 and 28 degrees of freedom. For each i, the probability that a central $F_{3,28}$ exceeds the number $\hat{F}_i$ shown in col. 3 is given in parentheses immediately below $\hat{F}_i$. The probabilities are very small. Suppose that consumer preferences are dependent on prices and total expenditure in accordance with (3.56), or — alternatively — suppose that consumer preferences are independent of prices and total expenditure in accordance with a still unknown direct utility function $V(X)$ that yields *additive logarithmic demand functions* (3.57). Then (it follows) that each of the values of the test statistics shown in col. 3 describes the occurrence of an extremely improbable event.

From the outcomes of the foregoing tests of significance we conclude that the stringent fixed preference hypothesis $H_0^{(1)}$, and both of the fixed preference compatible hypotheses $H_0^{(2)}$ and $H_0^{(3)}$ are discredited because their deductive implications are widely at variance with ascertained empirical fact.

3.5 Elasticities of Marginal Rates of Substitution

Rejection (Fisher, 1956, p. 35) of null hypotheses $H_0^{(1)}$, $H_0^{(2)}$ and $H_0^{(3)}$ leaves a still very broad class H_m^*

$$H_m^* = H_m - \left[H_0^{(1)} \cup H_0^{(2)} \cup H_0^{(3)} \right] \quad (3.61)$$

of alternative direct utility functions (3.2) that may be incorporated in the core of economic theory and used in the formation of related explanatory economic hypotheses. Acceptance of H_m^* as a paradigm of hypothesis formation calls attention to the special role of MRS-elasticities as fundamental determinants of the more familiar demand elasticities with respect to prices p_j and total expenditure M. Also, the central role played by the MRS-elasticities tends to focus attention on the matter of possible quantitative "laws" relating those elasticities to each other. Proffering such quantitative "laws" and testing them empirically is a normal science activity (Kuhn, 1962, p. 28) on which many hands need to be employed. It is beyond the scope of this book to describe such proffered quantitative "laws". However, the test of one time-honored hypothesis will be reported in this section.

Kalman (1968); Dusansky and Kalman (1972, 1974); Wichers, Dusansky, and Kalman (1976); Hayakawa (1976); and Liebhafsky (1980) have been concerned with general mathematical necessary and sufficient conditions for zero homogeneity of demand functions derived from utility functions whose parameters are dependent on prices and total expenditure. Accordingly we shall briefly examine the evidence in Table 3.1 that can be brought to bear on the question of zero homogeneity of marginal rates of substitution $R_i^{(k)}$, $i \neq k$.

Under the maintained hypothesis H_m, marginal rates of substitution $R_i^{(k)}$ are homogeneous functions of prices p_j and total expenditure, M; see equation (3.4). Let $\delta_i^{(k)}$ designate the degree of homogeneity of $R_i^{(k)}$ prices and total expenditure, i.e.,

$$\delta_i^{(k)} = \omega_{i0}^{(k)} + \sum_{j=1}^{n} \omega_{ij}^{(k)} \quad i \neq k. \tag{3.62}$$

Table 3.2 displays maximum likelihood estimates $\hat{\delta}_i^{(k)}$ of the degree $\delta_i^{(k)}$ of homogeneity of the marginal rates of substitution $R_i^{(k)}$. H_m implies that the $\delta_i^{(k)}$ satisfy the restrictions

$$\delta_k^{(i)} = -\delta_i^{(k)} \ \forall \ i,k \ i \neq k \tag{3.63}$$
$$\delta_i^{(k)} = -\delta_i^{(j)} - \delta_k^{(j)},$$

and the estimates $\hat{\delta}_i^{(k)}$ are forced to satisfy (3.63). Consequently, in view of (3.63) only 10 of the 20 $\hat{\delta}_i^{(k)}$ are shown in Table 3.2; and there are only 4 independent estimates $\hat{\delta}_i^{(k)}$.

For each $\hat{\delta}_i^{(k)}$, $i \neq k$, the corresponding F statistics is computed; under H_m and the hypothesis $\delta_i^{(k)} = 0$, the test statistic is distributed as a

	$\delta_i^{(1)}$	$\delta_i^{(2)}$	$\delta_i^{(3)}$	$\delta_i^{(4)}$	$\delta_i^{(5)}$
	TABLE 3.2				
	Maximum Likelihood Estimates of the Degree of				
	Homogeneity of MRS (See equation (3.7))				
1	-				
2	-2.247863	-			
	(.0020)				
3	1.813996	4.06185	-		
	(.1052)	(.0001)			
4	-8.33443	-6.086571	-10.148429	-	
	(.0001)	(.0001)	(.0001)		
5	-0.396068	1.851795	-2.210064	7.938365	-
	(.6372)	(.0267)	(.0147)	(.0003)	

central F variate with 1 and 28 degrees of freedom. The number shown in parentheses is the exact probability with which — given $\delta_i^{(k)} = 0$ — a central $F_{1,28}$ statistic exceeds the computed F statistic corresponding to $\hat{\delta}_i^{(k)}$.

Null hypothesis $H_0^{(4)}$ is characterized by the following restrictions on MRS-elasticities *wrt* total expenditure M and prices p_j:

$$\omega_{i0}^{(k)} + \sum_{j=1}^{n} \omega_{ij}^{(k)} = 0 \quad \forall \; i, k, \; i \neq k \tag{3.64}$$

$H_0^{(4)}$ implies that marginal rates of substitution (3.4) are homogeneous of degree zero in total expenditure M and prices p_j, i.e., $\delta_i^{(k)} = 0$. It follows too, from (3.64) that demand functions (3.12) and the behavior equations (3.13) are homogeneous of degree zero in prices and total expenditure.

Testing $\delta_i^{(k)} = 0$ one-by-one at (say) a level of significance commonly used, $\alpha = 0.05$, we can reject homogeneity of degree zero in nineteen cases. However, in view of the restrictions (3.63) not all of these cases are independent. A more balanced and precise appraisal of the relevant empirical evidence is obtained by confining attention to the basis S afforded by the $\hat{\delta}_i^{(i+1)}$ $i = 1, 2, \ldots, 4$, $\hat{\delta}_i^{(k)}$ appearing in the superdiagonal of Table 3.2. Every $\hat{\delta}_i^{(k)}$ in Table 3.2 is a definite linear function of $\hat{\delta}_i^{(i+1)}$ $i = 1, 2, \ldots, 4$, $\hat{\delta}_i^{(k)}$ in which the coefficients take on one of the magnitudes $-1, 0, 1$ and no others. At the $\alpha = 0.05$ level of significance usually chosen only two homogeneity subhypotheses $\delta_3^{(1)} = 0$ and $\delta_5^{(1)} = 0$ are not rejected; at the $\alpha = 0.50$ level of significance, only one of the homogeneity subhypotheses is not rejected.

Accept the estimates $\hat{\delta}_3^{(2)} = 4.061$ and $\hat{\delta}_2^{(1)} = -2.225$ for the time being. According to the first estimate if all prices and total expenditure increase equally by (say) the proportion μ, then the marginal rate of substitution $R_3^{(2)}$ of *clothing* for *housing* does not remain constant but increases by the proportion 4.061. According to the second estimate, under the same equal proportionate increase of prices and total expenditure, the marginal rate of substitution $R_2^{(1)}$ of food for clothing decreases by the proportion -2.225, or, equivalently, the marginal rate of substitution of clothing for housing increases by the proportion 0.518. On Veblen's interpretation[14] it appears that an equal proportionate increase in all prices and total expenditure tends to enhance the secondary utility of (the act of consuming) housing relative to the secondary utility of (the act of consuming) clothing; also that a general uniform rise in prices and ability to pay tends to enhance the secondary utility of (the act of consuming) clothing relative to the secondary utility of (the act of consuming) food. Possibly an increase in pecuniary means (quite apart from concurrent changes of prices) is accepted by consumers as a signal to review their tastes and preferences. An alternative explanation traceable to the beginnings of classical utility theory and the heyday of the hedonistic calculus is that consumers are deluded (in some unspecified way) into so regarding changes in their pecuniary means as a signal to review tastes and preferences, and that the supposed change in preferences consumers subsequently act upon is merely a phantasm; an appearance of a change that in reality never existed; a mere "money illusion." The hypotheses that the change of preferences is real is strongly resisted for a variety of methodological reasons, discussion of which is beyond the scope of this chapter; *cf.* Green (1978), p. 52; Friedman (1976), p. 207; Hansen (1970), pp 56-57, pp. 88-89; also Patinkin (1965), pp. 22-23.

Other quantitative "laws" relating MRS-elasticities can be conjectured of course, but such conjectures are likely to be the result of a systematic search of the elasticity estimates $\hat{\omega}_{i0}$ and $\hat{\omega}_{ij}$ for empirical regularities, a

---

[14]This is reviewed in Basmann, Molina and Slottje (1988)

normal science activity and a legitimate one if the same data are not employed to "test" the regularities discovered. To us it seems potentially more fruitful to search for empirical regularities in the MRS-elasticity estimates (and their anomalies) and, having found them, seek to explain the empirical regularities independently in terms of the physical properties of the commodities, consumer psychology, and interaction of consumer and commodity. For the sake of completeness, we present a basic set of maximum likelihood estimates of the MRS-elasticities under the maintained hypothesis H_m.

Table 3.3 displays maximum likelihood estimates $\hat{\omega}_{i0}^{(k)}$ of MRS-elasticities $\omega_{i0}^{(k)}$ $i, j = 1, 2, \ldots, 5$, *wrt* total expenditure, M, under the maintained hypothesis H_m, (3.13). Since the estimates satisfy the skew symmetry condition (3.9) implied by H_m, we show only the $\hat{\omega}_{i0}^{(k)}$ for $i > k$, although all $\hat{\omega}_{i0}^{(k)}$ $i \neq k$ were independently computed. For each $\hat{\omega}_{i0}^{(k)}$ $i \neq k$ the corresponding t-statistic was computed; under H_m and the hypotheses $\omega_{i0}^{(k)} = 0$, the t-statistic $\hat{t}_{i0}^{(k)}$, is distributed exactly as Students-t with 28 degrees of freedom. In Table 3.3 the number in parenthesis is the exact probability that $|t|$ exceeds $|\hat{t}_{i0}^{(k)}|$ calculated from the sample if $\omega_{i0}^{(k)} = 0$.

Notice that only four of the ten estimates $\hat{\omega}_{i0}^{(k)}$ in Table 3.3 are independent since they satisfy the condition (3.9).

$$\hat{\omega}_{i0}^{(k)} = \hat{\omega}_{i0}^{(j)} - \hat{\omega}_{k0}^{(j)}. \tag{3.65}$$

In consequence of (3.65) it follows that the ranking of MRS-elasticities *wrt* total expenditure, $\omega_{i0}^{(k)}$ $i = 1, 2, \ldots, n$, in order of descending magnitude is invariant against change of numeraire, k. For the commodity groups used in this study, the MRS-elasticity for durables $(i = 4)$ $\hat{\omega}_{40}^{(k)}$ is greatest for every numeraire $k \neq 4$; the MRS-elasticity for medical services $(i = 5)$ is least for every numeraire $k \neq 5$. The invariance of these rankings is not significant empirical information, of course; but the fact that the durables composite is first and the medical services composite is last in the rank order is empirical information of some considerable significance in the light of some generalizations of Veblen's concerning the relative abilities of different kinds of commodities to serve the needs of conspicuous consumption.

In a general way, at least, the MRS-elasticities *wrt* M for those commodities whose ownership or consumption is highly visible to the com-

TABLE 3.3
Maximum Likelihood Estimates of MRS-Elasticities
wrt M (See equation (3.7)

	$\omega_{i0}^{(1)}$	$\omega_{i0}^{(2)}$	$\omega_{i0}^{(3)}$	$\omega_{i0}^{(4)}$	$\omega_{i0}^{(5)}$
1	-				
2	0.492221	-			
3	0.101492	0.390729	-		
	(.16883)	(.1159)			
4	2.135456	1.643235	2.033964	-	
	(.0001)	(.0001)	(.0001)		
5	0.369397	-0.122824	0.267905	-1.766059	-
	(.0371)	(.4527)	(.1773)	(.0001)	

munity tend to be large *cf.* Veblen, 1899, p. 112. On the other hand, commodities whose consumption is usually screened from public view (Veblen, 1899, pp. 113-115) or whose consumption represents an archaic or obsolescent form of conspicuous waste or demonstration of one's leisure class status *e.g.*, the consumption of medical services tend to have MRS-elasticities *wrt* total expenditure that are in the lower ranks in Table 3.3.

Table 3.4 displays maximum-likelihood estimates $\hat{\omega}_{jj}^{(k)}$ of own price MRS-elasticities $\hat{\omega}_{jj}^{(k)}$ $j, k = 1, 2, \ldots, 5$, *wrt* prices p_j under the maintained hypothesis H_m, (3.10). Since the estimates $\hat{\omega}_{ij}^{(k)}$ satisfy the constraints (3.10), estimates of the cross-price MRS elasticities can be computed from Table 3.4 by means of the formula

$$\hat{\omega}_{ij}^{(k)} = \hat{\omega}_{jj}^{(k)} - \hat{\omega}_{jj}^{(i)} \quad i \neq j \tag{3.66}$$

For each $\hat{\omega}_{jj}^{(k)}$, $j \neq k$, the corresponding t-statistic, $\hat{t}_{jj}^{(k)}$, was computed. Under H_m and the hypothesis $\omega_{jj}^{(k)} = 0$, the t-statistic is distributed as Student's t with 28 degrees of freedom. In each cell of Table 3.4 the number in parentheses is the exact probability that $|t| > |\hat{t}_{jj}^{(k)}|$ under the hypothesis $\omega_{jj}^{(k)} = 0$.

If hypotheses to the effect that own-price MRS elasticities $\omega_{jj}^{(k)} = 0$ are tested one-by-one at a level of significance that is extremely risk averse to "rejecting" '$\omega_{jj}^{(k)} = 0$' when that hypothesis holds, then the significant own-price MRS-elasticity estimates $\hat{\omega}_{jj}^{(k)}$ are substantial in number and all are

		TABLE 3.4			
		Maximum Likelihood Estimates of Own MRS- Elasticities			
		(See equation (3.10))			
(numer.)	$\omega_{jj}^{(1)}$	$\omega_{jj}^{(2)}$	$\omega_{jj}^{(3)}$	$\omega_{jj}^{(4)}$	$\omega_{jj}^{(5)}$
1	-	0.516504	0.518711	1.413514	0.671852
		(.0028)	(.1027)	(.0001)	(.0031)
2	0.297755	-	1.298856	1.04004	0.536844
	(.1733)		(.0030)	(.0206)	(.0548)
3	0.674098	0.718585	-	-0.345741	0.932903
	(.0911)	(.0626)		(.3990)	(.0040)
4	-0.09188	0.99467	1.010196	-	-0.072769
	(.7904)	(.7707)	(.9768)		(.8293)
5	1.024408	1.200592	-0.00808456	2.386577	-

positive with the exception of four which are all statistically insignificant. For instance, if the level of significance selected is $\alpha = 0.01$, then 8 of the 20 own-price MRS-elasticity estimates are significant and all of them are positive. If the level of significance is the more usual but still risk averse $\alpha = 0.05$, then 10 of the 20 own-price MRS-elasticity estimates $\hat{\omega}_{jj}^{(k)}$ are significant. Clearly then, by using dynamic preference formation (which is dependent on commodity prices and total expenditure) as a maintained hypothesis, the neo-classical theory of the consumer is in excellent agreement with post-second world war commodity group price and expenditure data for the United States. We now summarize the chapter.

3.6   Chapter Summary

This chapter presented empirical tests of direct utility functions that rationalized systems of demand functions that have the Slutsky property. The maintained hypothesis analyzed here was that consumers maximize a direct utility function having a generalized Fechner-Thurstone form subject only to the ordinary budget constraint. The outcomes of the tests performed indicated that generalized Fechner-Thurstone direct utility functions that are compatible with fixed preferences were strongly rejected against the alternatives. The rejection of the three forms tested still left a very broad class of alternative direct utility functions of the generalized

Fechner-Thurstone form that are dependent on prices and total expenditure. As section four of the chapter demonstrated, if Thorstein Veblen's explanatory theory of utility and dynamic preference formation is adopted as a maintained hypothesis, the new-classical theory is in excellent agreement with post-second world war commodity expenditure data for the United States.

Chapter 4

The GFT and Alternative Forms

4.1 Introduction

In the last chapter we showed explicitly how the GFT-direct utility function yields empirically testable hypotheses. Since Cournot, Dupuit and Gossen first laid out what evolved into the modern theory of consumer demand (predicated on the concept of individual utility maximization) a hundred and fifty years ago, virtually hundreds of articles have been written attempting to explicate and measure the theory *cf.* Stigler (1954). Among the modern contributors, Stone (1954), Houthakker (1960), Theil (1967), Christensen, Jorgenson and Lau (1975), Deaton and Muellbauer (1980a) and Basmann, Molina and Slottje (1983) have all introduced explicit demand functions to test the theory. Some have based their demand systems on explicit utility functions, some have not.

The purpose of this chapter is to demonstrate that observationally equivalent images of all of these functional forms are nested within the GFT form and that we can evaluate each of these observationally equivalent images against the GFT by analyzing the likelihood support of each model. The GFT form has been defined previously in chapter one and again in section 2.4 but section 4.2 below will remind the reader of its' important attributes. We demonstrate its relation to the other forms and we present the empirical results in section 4.3 and conclude the study in section 4.4.

4.2   Fechner and Thurstone Revisited

In this book we have focussed on the Generalized Fechner Thurstone direct
Utility Function. The names Fechner and Thurstone were chosen for this
utility function since L. L. Thurstone was probably the first to study
indifference maps experimentally and G. Fechner's famous logarithmic law
suggested a weighted geometric mean of quantities of commodities as a
useful form of direct utility function. We have noted that to write the
GFT utility function, let $p = (p_1, \ldots, p_n)$ be a vector of positive prices and
assume that consumers allocate nominal income, M, to the purchase of
commodities $X = (X_1, \ldots, X_n)$ in accordance with the usual linear budget
constraint:

$$\sum_{k=1}^{n} p_k X_k = M \tag{4.1}$$

This allocative behavior necessarily results in maximization of a direct
utility function having the form (*cf.*, chapter one)

$$U(X; \theta) = \prod_{i=1}^{n} (X_i - \gamma_i)^{\theta_i}, \tag{4.2}$$

where:

$$
\begin{aligned}
X_i &> \max\{0, \gamma_i\}, \\
\theta_i = \theta_i^*(p, M; \Psi)e^{u_i} &> 0, \quad i = 1, 2, \ldots, n, \\
\theta &= \sum_{i=1}^{n} \theta_i
\end{aligned}
\tag{4.3}
$$

At first glance the GFT form looks like a Cobb-Douglas form of production function, but the differences are important as noted by Samuelson and
Sato (1984). The first difference is that the exponents θ_i are, in general,
dependent on p and M and in our model we include an additional variable,
Ψ, with θ_i^* as the equilibrium value of θ_i. The Cobb-Douglas utility function specifies the exponents of the utility function to be constants and not
functions of p, M, Ψ, or u. Actually it was Thurstone (1931) who first used
the constant weight form of utility function with Cobb and Douglas working with production functions. The reason why the Fechner-Thurstone

utility function is prefixed "generalized" is to alert the reader that the exponents are dependent on other variables. A similar line of research is developed by Pollak (1977) where it is shown that a fixed coefficient price dependent preference ordering can rationalize any demand system that does not contain inferior goods. The GFT direct utility function contains no restriction on the normality or inferiority of goods and rationalizes all the same demand systems rationalized by the fixed coefficient price dependent model. In empirical applications of the GFT function, Ψ is a vector of specified observable nonstochastic variables on which consumers' indifference maps depend. In many cases, γ represents a vector of subsistence levels of the commodities X_i, but $\gamma = 0$ is assumed with no loss in generality. The latent random vector $u = (u_1, \ldots, u_n)$ has a zero mean vector and finite positive definite matrix W_0 and represents stochastic changes in tastes. Variations of the stochastic taste changer u produce changes in marginal rates of substitution between commodities, in the curvature of indifference curves, and higher derivatives. However, stochastic taste changers do not destroy the convexity of indifference curves. The chief theoretical properties of u are discussed in Basmann (1985) and the actual estimation of serial correlation hypotheses has been outlined in sections 3.3.1 and 3.3.2.

The statement, "if consumers allocate their income in accordance with the linear budget constraint, then they must maximize the GFT utility function" will seem peculiar to some readers. The sense in which the above holds is that, given any system of demand functions rationalized by a "standard" utility function, the parameters of the GFT weights (θ_i) can be uniquely determined such that the resulting GFT utility function yields exactly the same system of demand functions as the "standard" utility functions. In other words, the GFT is more general than the "standard" utility forms since a GFT utility function can rationalize any system of demand functions derived from any of the standard utility forms. For the details of constructing the exponent functions from any price and expenditure data, see Basmann *et al.* (1983, 1984b, esp. Sect. II). Notice, too, that it is not asserted that consumers intend to maximize the GFT utility function which is unimportant anyway and discussed by Samuelson (1947, p. 23) who pointed out that the principle of maximizing behavior does not entail the assumption that the maximizing behavior is purposive, or that the consumers are aware they are maximizing any function.

It is emphasized here that only the commodities X_i are arguments of the GFT direct utility function. The exponents θ_i of commodities X_i are not specified to be constants and each depends in part on a random magnitude u_i. In some applications the exponents θ_i are functions of the vector p of n budget constraint prices, total expenditure M, and other systematic magnitudes, $\Psi_i, \ldots, \Psi_q$, as well as of u_i. Thus, u, Ψ, p and M may be arguments of the exponent functions θ_i but they are not arguments of the GFT utility function. With the theoretical basis described, we return now to comparing this form of direct utility function to alternative specifications.

4.3   Empirical Results

As noted above, the likelihood support for modeling aggregate consumer behavior in the context of alternative neo-classical model specifications which have images within the GFT-CEMRS class are investigated. Minimal sufficient statistics for each empirical model are estimated using the General Linear Model (GLM). The theory underlying specification of serial correlation hypotheses on random preference changers is given in the article by Basmann (1985). The dependent variable vector and the matrix of independent variables are transformed according to a given serial correlation hypotheses. The GLS estimators are obtained by applying the method of least squares to the transformed model as is outlined in section 3.3.

Alternative models referenced in this chapter will be noted as follows:

1. GFT-CEMRS Unrestricted.

$$\ln \frac{M_i}{M_n} = \ln \frac{\beta_i}{\beta_n} + \omega_{i0}^{(n)} \ln M + \sum_{j=1}^{n} \omega_{ij}^{(n)} \ln p_j + \eta_i^{(n)} \qquad (4.4)$$

$$i = 1, \ldots, 4 \quad n = 5$$

2. Cobb-Douglas: (GFT-CEMRS class)

$$\ln \frac{M_i}{M_n} = \ln \frac{\beta_i}{\beta_n} + \eta_i^{(n)} \qquad (4.5)$$

$$i = 1, \ldots, 4 \quad n = 5$$

3. Leontief: (GFT-CEMRS class)

$$\ln \frac{M_i}{M_n} = \ln \frac{\beta_i}{\beta_n} + \omega_{ii}^{(n)} \ln p_i + \omega_{in}^{(n)} \ln p_n + \eta_i^{(n)} \qquad (4.6)$$

$$i,j = 1,\ldots,4 \quad i \neq n$$

with restrictions

$$\omega_{in}^{(n)} + \omega_{ii}^{(n)} = 0$$

$$\omega_{ii}^{(n)} = 1$$

4. Relaxed CES: (GFT-CEMRS class)

$$\ln \frac{M_i}{M_n} = \ln \frac{\beta_i}{\beta_n} + \omega_{ii}^{(n)} \ln p_i + \omega_{in}^{(n)} \ln p_n + \eta_i^{(n)} \qquad (4.7)$$

$$i,j = 1,\ldots,4 \quad i \neq n$$

with restrictions

$$\omega_{in}^{(n)} = \omega_{jn}^{(n)}$$

5. CES: (GFT-CEMRS class)

$$\ln \frac{M_i}{M_n} = \ln \frac{\beta_i}{\beta_n} + \omega_{ii}^{(n)} \ln p_i + \omega_{in}^{(n)} \ln p_n + \eta_i^{(n)} \qquad (4.8)$$

$$i,j = 1,\ldots,4 \quad i \neq n$$

with restrictions

$$\omega_{ii}^{(n)} + \omega_{in}^{(n)} = 0$$

6. Leser - Houthakker: (GFT-CEMRS class)

$$\ln \frac{M_i}{M_n} = \ln \frac{\beta_i}{\beta_n} + \omega_{i0}^{(n)} \ln M + \omega_{ii}^{(n)} \ln p_i + \omega_{in}^{(n)} \ln p_n + \eta_i^{(n)}$$

$$i,j = 1,\ldots,4 \quad i \neq n \qquad (4.9)$$

with restrictions

$$\omega_{in}^{(n)} = \omega_{jn}^{(n)}$$

$$\omega_{i0}^{(n)} + \omega_{ii}^{(n)} + \omega_{in}^{(n)} = 0$$

$$\omega_{ii}^{(n)} < 1 \quad \omega_{in}^{(n)} > -1$$

For each $i = 1, \ldots, (n-1)$ the random element, $\eta_i^{(n)}$ in each estimation equation satisfies the serial correlation hypotheses outlined in section 3.3.1 above.

As was mentioned in section 3.3.2 above a grid search method was utilized to evaluate the likelihood support for fifty pairs of autocorrelation parameters ϕ_1 and ϕ_2 which were specified to line within the unit circle of the complex plan so as to satisfy the routhian conditions for stability as outlined in section 3.3.1. Likelihood ratios were evaluated for each $AR(2)$ specification relative to the $AR(2)$ specification which generated the largest likelihood value as follows:

$$\ddot{\lambda}_{\phi_1, \phi_2} = \frac{L(\hat{B}, \hat{\Sigma}; X | \phi_1 = \phi_{1(0)}, \phi_2 = \phi_{2(0)})}{L_{max}(\hat{B}, \hat{\Sigma}; X | \phi_1 = \phi_{1(0)}, \phi_2 = \phi_{2(0)})} \qquad (4.10)$$

Likelihood support evaluated over the AR(1) stability grid for model 1 are presented in Tables 4.1 and 4.2.

Hypothesis tests between restricted and unrestricted models within a specified GFT class were performed using a likelihood ratio test as a procedure as outlined in section 3.3.1 along with Mood, Graybill, and Boes (1974), and Graybill (1976). The likelihood ratio test statistic is defined as follows:

$$\lambda_{\phi_1, \phi_2} = \frac{L(restricted \, | \phi_1 = \phi_{1(0)}, \phi_2 = \phi_{2(0)})}{L(unrestricted \, | \phi_1 = \phi_{1(0)}, \phi_2 = \phi_{2(0)})} \qquad (4.11)$$

The test statistic $-2 \ln \lambda_{\phi_1, \phi_2}$ is distributed as chi-square with r degrees of freedom.

Model 2 through model 7 are tested within the GFT-CEMRS class specified by model 1. Tables 4.1–4.5 contain the values for the computed likelihood ratio test statistic $-2 \ln \lambda_{\phi_1, \phi_2}$, evaluated for each $AR(2)$ hypothesis along with the approximate chi-square value associated with each test. In addition the a p-value associated with the chi-square distribution for each test is included, where a small value suggests rejection of the restricted model.

4.4   Chapter Summary

As can be seen by examining Tables 4.1-4.5, the likelihood support for any of the alternative forms against the GFT-Class is very close to zero

$(0.00 * 10^{-25})$ or more. Our results (which are discussed in subsequent chapters) indicate that the GFT-direct Utility Function and its implied model of aggregate consumer behavior is in excellent agreement with post-world war II data. For the class of utility functions whose GFT-equivalents were discussed above, we can unfortunately not make the same claim.[1]

---

[1] An expanded version of this chapter including other classes of functional forms is currently being written (Basmann, Johnson and Slottje (1988b), see also Fawson and Johnson (1988)).

TABLE 4.1					
Likelihood Ratio Test of Cobb Douglas against					
GFT-CEMRS alternative					
ϕ_1	ϕ_2	$|\hat{\Sigma}(unrestrict.)|$	$|\hat{\Sigma}(restricted)|$	$-T\ln\frac{|\hat{\Sigma}(restricted)|}{|\hat{\Sigma}(unrestrict.)|}$	$prob\chi^2_{35df}$
-1.5	0.75	2.9995E-18	2.0803E-09	590.362	0
-1.25	0.75	7.7072E-19	8.6867E-10	604.444	0
-1	0.75	2.2218E-19	3.3645E-10	613.008	0
-0.75	0.75	8.5125E-20	1.1954E-10	610.821	0
-0.5	0.75	4.9728E-20	3.8499E-11	593.553	0
-0.25	0.75	4.6600E-20	1.1121E-11	559.426	0
0	0.75	6.1796E-20	2.8677E-12	511.936	0
0.25	0.75	9.4085E-20	6.6688E-13	457.444	0
0.5	0.75	1.3660E-19	1.4519E-13	402.42	0
0.75	0.75	1.7224E-19	3.1732E-14	351.595	0
1	0.75	1.8815E-19	7.4813E-15	307.13	0
1.25	0.75	1.9587E-19	1.7973E-15	264.606	0
1.5	0.75	1.5626E-19	2.8478E-16	217.731	0
-1.25	0.5	1.2214E-18	4.8540E-10	574.215	0
-1	0.5	3.4724E-19	1.7799E-10	581.594	0
-0.75	0.5	1.2418E-19	5.9284E-11	579.532	0
-0.5	0.5	6.3720E-20	1.7690E-11	563.812	0
-0.25	0.5	4.8767E-20	4.6708E-12	532.948	0
0	0.5	5.2123E-20	1.0855E-12	488.699	0
0.25	0.5	6.6365E-20	2.2509E-13	436.068	0
0.5	0.5	8.5643E-20	4.3727E-14	381.156	0
0.75	0.5	1.0396E-19	8.6680E-15	328.604	0
1	0.5	1.2194E-19	1.8177E-15	278.677	0
1.25	0.5	1.2906E-19	3.0970E-16	225.709	0
-1	0.25	6.3891E-19	9.4574E-11	545.574	0
-0.75	0.25	2.2114E-19	2.9654E-11	542.708	0
-0.5	0.25	1.0201E-19	8.2560E-12	528.064	0
-0.25	0.25	6.6384E-20	2.0161E-12	499.641	0
0	0.25	5.8608E-20	4.3079E-13	458.498	0
0.25	0.25	6.3261E-20	8.2239E-14	408.258	0
0.5	0.25	7.5022E-20	1.4857E-14	353.689	0
0.75	0.25	9.3214E-20	2.7008E-15	297.951	0
1	0.25	1.1516E-19	4.4526E-16	239.543	0
-0.75	0	4.2550E-19	1.5090E-11	504.137	0
-0.5	0	1.8236E-19	3.9614E-12	489.923	0
-0.25	0	1.0415E-19	9.0988E-13	463.506	0
0	0	7.9820E-20	1.8330E-13	424.759	0
0.25	0	7.7654E-20	3.3209E-14	376.016	0
0.5	0	8.9364E-20	5.6338E-15	320.496	0
0.75	0	1.1299E-19	8.7402E-16	259.654	0
-0.5	-0.25	3.5166E-19	1.9698E-12	450.618	0
-0.25	-0.25	1.8645E-19	4.3227E-13	425.036	0
0	-0.25	1.3058E-19	8.3426E-14	387.657	0
0.25	-0.25	1.1922E-19	1.4357E-14	339.265	0
0.5	-0.25	1.3341E-19	2.1947E-15	281.536	0
-0.25	-0.5	3.7376E-19	2.1412E-13	384.495	0
0	-0.5	2.5081E-19	3.9433E-14	346.997	0
0.25	-0.5	2.1853E-19	6.3033E-15	297.821	0
0	-0.75	5.3842E-19	1.8825E-14	303.399	0

		TABLE 4.2			
		Likelihood Ratio Test of Leontief against			
		GFT-CEMRS alternative			
ϕ_1	ϕ_2	$|\hat{\Sigma}(unrestrict.)|$	$|\hat{\Sigma}(restricted)|$	$-T\ln\frac{|\hat{\Sigma}(restricted)|}{|\hat{\Sigma}(unrestrict.)|}$	$\mathrm{prob}\chi^2_{35df}$
-1.5	0.75	2.9995E-18	7.6906E-09	628.279	0
-1.25	0.75	7.7072E-19	3.1904E-09	642.171	0
-1	0.75	2.2218E-19	1.2676E-09	651.475	0
-0.75	0.75	8.5125E-20	4.8623E-10	651.509	0
-0.5	0.75	4.9728E-20	1.8177E-10	638.563	0
-0.25	0.75	4.6600E-20	6.6621E-11	611.34	0
0	0.75	6.1796E-20	2.3912E-11	573.441	0
0.25	0.75	9.4085E-20	8.3693E-12	530.806	0
0.5	0.75	1.3660E-19	2.8521E-12	488.775	0
0.75	0.75	1.7224E-19	9.3101E-13	449.585	0
1	0.75	1.8815E-19	2.7054E-13	411.183	0
1.25	0.75	1.9587E-19	6.0572E-14	366.615	0
1.5	0.75	1.5626E-19	8.1743E-15	315.085	0
-1.25	0.5	1.2214E-18	1.9174E-09	614.053	0
-1	0.5	3.4724E-19	7.1367E-10	621.866	0
-0.75	0.5	1.2418E-19	2.5278E-10	621.587	0
-0.5	0.5	6.3720E-20	8.5999E-11	609.67	0
-0.25	0.5	4.8767E-20	2.8332E-11	585.226	0
0	0.5	5.2123E-20	9.0537E-12	550.212	0
0.25	0.5	6.6365E-20	2.7956E-12	509.128	0
0.5	0.5	8.5643E-20	8.2655E-13	466.395	0
0.75	0.5	1.0396E-19	2.2480E-13	423.016	0
1	0.5	1.2194E-19	5.0684E-14	375.19	0
1.25	0.5	1.2906E-19	7.9570E-15	319.849	0
-1	0.25	6.3891E-19	4.2059E-10	588.85	0
-0.75	0.25	2.2114E-19	1.3897E-10	587.503	0
-0.5	0.25	1.0201E-19	4.3409E-11	576.196	0
-0.25	0.25	6.6384E-20	1.2924E-11	553.52	0
0	0.25	5.8608E-20	3.6780E-12	520.688	0
0.25	0.25	6.3261E-20	9.9313E-13	480.504	0
0.5	0.25	7.5022E-20	2.4789E-13	435.31	0
0.75	0.25	9.3214E-20	5.3765E-14	384.692	0
1	0.25	1.1516E-19	9.1960E-15	327.351	0
-0.75	0	4.2550E-19	8.0607E-11	552.728	0
-0.5	0	1.8236E-19	2.3383E-11	541.409	0
-0.25	0	1.0415E-19	6.3391E-12	519.8	0
0	0	7.9820E-20	1.6042E-12	487.668	0
0.25	0	7.7654E-20	3.7285E-13	446.149	0
0.5	0	8.9364E-20	7.6739E-14	396.233	0
0.75	0	1.1299E-19	1.3419E-14	338.862	0
-0.5	-0.25	3.5166E-19	1.3184E-11	505.749	0
-0.25	-0.25	1.8645E-19	3.2657E-12	483.679	0
0	-0.25	1.3058E-19	7.3159E-13	450.624	0
0.25	-0.25	1.1922E-19	1.4551E-13	406.43	0
0.5	-0.25	1.3341E-19	2.5426E-14	352.578	0
-0.25	-0.5	3.7376E-19	1.7150E-12	444.834	0
0	-0.5	2.5081E-19	3.4266E-13	409.699	0
0.25	-0.5	2.1853E-19	6.0667E-14	363.486	0
0	-0.75	5.3842E-19	1.6884E-13	367.019	0

			TABLE 4.3		
			Likelihood Ratio Test of Relaxed CES against		
			GFT-CEMRS alternative		
ϕ_1	ϕ_2	$|\hat{\Sigma}(unrestrict.)|$	$|\hat{\Sigma}(restricted)|$	$-T\ln\frac{|\hat{\Sigma}(restricted)|}{|\hat{\Sigma}(unrestrict.)|}$	$\mathrm{prob}\chi^2_{29df}$
-1.5	0.75	2.9995E-18	1.5124E-08	647.891	0
-1.25	0.75	7.7072E-19	6.9815E-09	664.882	0
-1	0.75	2.2218E-19	2.9962E-09	676.421	0
-0.75	0.75	8.5125E-20	1.1507E-09	676.491	0
-0.5	0.75	4.9728E-20	3.8472E-10	660.307	0
-0.25	0.75	4.6600E-20	1.1621E-10	627.475	0
0	0.75	6.1796E-20	3.2529E-11	582.365	0
0.25	0.75	9.4085E-20	8.0707E-12	529.752	0
0.5	0.75	1.3660E-19	1.8498E-12	476.219	0
0.75	0.75	1.7224E-19	4.1711E-13	426.3	0
1	0.75	1.8815E-19	8.0527E-14	376.04	0
1.25	0.75	1.9587E-19	7.5339E-15	306.167	0
1.5	0.75	1.5626E-19	1.0523E-16	188.86	0
-1.25	0.5	1.2214E-18	3.5158E-09	631.636	0
-1	0.5	3.4724E-19	1.4130E-09	641.675	0
-0.75	0.5	1.2418E-19	5.0519E-10	641.667	0
-0.5	0.5	6.3720E-20	1.5651E-10	627.034	0
-0.25	0.5	4.8767E-20	4.2358E-11	596.888	0
0	0.5	5.2123E-20	1.0040E-11	553.21	0
0.25	0.5	6.6365E-20	2.0798E-12	500.551	0
0.5	0.5	8.5643E-20	3.9865E-13	445.249	0
0.75	0.5	1.0396E-19	6.9334E-14	388.904	0
1	0.5	1.2194E-19	7.4819E-15	319.71	0
1.25	0.5	1.2906E-19	1.8146E-16	210.207	0
-1	0.25	6.3891E-19	6.3988E-10	601.019	0
-0.75	0.25	2.2114E-19	2.1247E-10	599.815	0
-0.5	0.25	1.0201E-19	6.0282E-11	585.718	0
-0.25	0.25	6.6384E-20	1.4323E-11	556.5	0
0	0.25	5.8608E-20	2.8540E-12	513.332	0
0.25	0.25	6.3261E-20	4.9231E-13	460.153	0
0.5	0.25	7.5022E-20	7.4960E-14	400.626	0
0.75	0.25	9.3214E-20	8.2122E-15	330.201	0
1	0.25	1.1516E-19	3.0499E-16	228.57	0
-0.75	0	4.2550E-19	8.3667E-11	553.808	0
-0.5	0	1.8236E-19	2.1458E-11	538.918	0
-0.25	0	1.0415E-19	4.4849E-12	509.765	0
0	0	7.9820E-20	7.6347E-13	466.135	0
0.25	0	7.7654E-20	1.0793E-13	410.198	0
0.5	0	8.9364E-20	1.1475E-14	341.125	0
0.75	0	1.1299E-19	5.5705E-16	246.591	0
-0.5	-0.25	3.5166E-19	7.0950E-12	487.78	0
-0.25	-0.25	1.8645E-19	1.3153E-12	457.305	0
0	-0.25	1.3058E-19	1.9218E-13	411.857	0
0.25	-0.25	1.1922E-19	2.0686E-14	349.857	0
0.5	-0.25	1.3341E-19	1.1950E-15	263.907	0
-0.25	-0.5	3.7376E-19	3.6636E-13	400.07	0
0	-0.5	2.5081E-19	4.3106E-14	349.58	0
0.25	-0.5	2.1853E-19	2.9263E-15	275.568	0
0	-0.75	5.3842E-19	7.4441E-15	276.495	0

TABLE 4.4
Likelihood Ratio Test of CES against
GFT-CEMRS alternative

ϕ_1	ϕ_2	$|\hat{\Sigma}(unrestrict.)|$	$|\hat{\Sigma}(restricted)|$	$-T\ln\frac{|\hat{\Sigma}(restricted)|}{|\hat{\Sigma}(unrestrict.)|}$	$\text{prob}\chi^2_{30df}$
-1.5	0.75	2.9995E-18	2.4647E-08	662.054	0
-1.25	0.75	7.7072E-19	1.1389E-08	679.073	0
-1	0.75	2.2218E-19	5.0930E-09	691.806	0
-0.75	0.75	8.5125E-20	2.1271E-09	694.308	0
-0.5	0.75	4.9728E-20	7.5718E-10	679.942	0
-0.25	0.75	4.6600E-20	2.2501E-10	646.637	0
0	0.75	6.1796E-20	5.9049E-11	599.656	0
0.25	0.75	9.4085E-20	1.3268E-11	544.168	0
0.5	0.75	1.3660E-19	2.5604E-12	485.645	0
0.75	0.75	1.7224E-19	4.4907E-13	428.441	0
1	0.75	1.8815E-19	7.2714E-14	373.08	0
1.25	0.75	1.9587E-19	7.7908E-15	307.139	0
1.5	0.75	1.5626E-19	2.3424E-16	212.065	0
-1.25	0.5	1.2214E-18	6.4955E-09	649.438	0
-1	0.5	3.4724E-19	2.6802E-09	660.239	0
-0.75	0.5	1.2418E-19	1.0012E-09	661.504	0
-0.5	0.5	6.3720E-20	3.2211E-10	647.966	0
-0.25	0.5	4.8767E-20	8.6991E-11	617.759	0
0	0.5	5.2123E-20	1.9640E-11	572.669	0
0.25	0.5	6.6365E-20	3.6578E-12	516.924	0
0.5	0.5	8.5643E-20	5.7924E-13	456.084	0
0.75	0.5	1.0396E-19	8.0571E-14	393.26	0
1	0.5	1.2194E-19	8.3739E-15	322.976	0
1.25	0.5	1.2906E-19	3.2937E-16	227.495	0
-1	0.25	6.3891E-19	1.3256E-09	622.142	0
-0.75	0.25	2.2114E-19	4.5357E-10	621.807	0
-0.5	0.25	1.0201E-19	1.3145E-10	608.327	0
-0.25	0.25	6.6384E-20	3.1238E-11	579.114	0
0	0.25	5.8608E-20	6.0157E-12	534.956	0
0.25	0.25	6.3261E-20	9.4035E-13	478.92	0
0.5	0.25	7.5022E-20	1.2072E-13	414.444	0
0.75	0.25	9.3214E-20	1.1628E-14	340.286	0
1	0.25	1.1516E-19	5.4941E-16	245.638	0
-0.75	0	4.2550E-19	1.8578E-10	576.943	0
-0.5	0	1.8236E-19	4.8626E-11	562.642	0
-0.25	0	1.0415E-19	1.0243E-11	533.715	0
0	0	7.9820E-20	1.7067E-12	489.464	0
0.25	0	7.7654E-20	2.2225E-13	431.144	0
0.5	0	8.9364E-20	2.1010E-14	358.666	0
0.75	0	1.1299E-19	1.1274E-15	267.037	0
-0.5	-0.25	3.5166E-19	1.6171E-11	511.67	0
-0.25	-0.25	1.8645E-19	3.0413E-12	481.614	0
0	-0.25	1.3058E-19	4.3926E-13	435.83	0
0.25	-0.25	1.1922E-19	4.5213E-14	372.533	0
0.5	-0.25	1.3341E-19	2.8391E-15	289.001	0
-0.25	-0.5	3.7376E-19	8.4234E-13	424.214	0
0	-0.5	2.5081E-19	1.0224E-13	374.627	0
0.25	-0.5	2.1853E-19	7.9510E-15	304.555	0
0	-0.75	5.3842E-19	2.2117E-14	308.073	0

		TABLE 4.5 Likelihood Ratio Test of Leser Houthakker against GFT-CEMRS alternative			
ϕ_1	ϕ_2	$\|\hat{\Sigma}(unrestrict.)\|$	$\|\hat{\Sigma}(restricted)\|$	$-T\ln\frac{\|\hat{\Sigma}(restricted)\|}{\|\hat{\Sigma}(unrestrict.)\|}$	$prob\chi^2_{29df}$
-1.5	0.75	2.9995E-18	8.6375E-11	498.097	0
-1.25	0.75	7.7072E-19	4.1970E-11	516.574	0
-1	0.75	2.2218E-19	1.7020E-11	526.47	0
-0.75	0.75	8.5125E-20	5.5676E-12	521.887	0
-0.5	0.75	4.9728E-20	1.5314E-12	500.044	0
-0.25	0.75	4.6600E-20	4.7040E-13	467.697	0
0	0.75	6.1796E-20	1.9687E-13	434.252	0
0.25	0.75	9.4085E-20	8.0698E-14	396.199	0
0.5	0.75	1.3660E-19	2.8672E-14	355.378	0
0.75	0.75	1.7224E-19	7.9785E-15	311.558	0
1	0.75	1.8815E-19	1.7935E-15	265.711	0
1.25	0.75	1.9587E-19	3.8527E-16	219.944	0
1.5	0.75	1.5626E-19	7.7766E-17	180.088	0
-1.25	0.5	1.2214E-18	1.6410E-11	475.99	0
-1	0.5	3.4724E-19	6.0402E-12	483.479	0
-0.75	0.5	1.2418E-19	1.8459E-12	478.921	0
-0.5	0.5	6.3720E-20	5.3740E-13	462.485	0
-0.25	0.5	4.8767E-20	1.8949E-13	440.01	0
0	0.5	5.2123E-20	7.7187E-14	412.036	0
0.25	0.5	6.6365E-20	2.9529E-14	377.165	0
0.5	0.5	8.5643E-20	9.2850E-15	336.218	0
0.75	0.5	1.0396E-19	2.2604E-15	289.625	0
1	0.5	1.2194E-19	4.6711E-16	239.273	0
1.25	0.5	1.2906E-19	8.8638E-17	189.429	0
-1	0.25	6.3891E-19	2.7473E-12	442.95	0
-0.75	0.25	2.2114E-19	8.4553E-13	439.544	0
-0.5	0.25	1.0201E-19	2.6562E-13	428.401	0
-0.25	0.25	6.6384E-20	9.4493E-14	410.889	0
0	0.25	5.8608E-20	3.5400E-14	386.029	0
0.25	0.25	6.3261E-20	1.2058E-14	352.581	0
0.5	0.25	7.5022E-20	3.3514E-15	310.506	0
0.75	0.25	9.3214E-20	7.5239E-16	260.887	0
1	0.25	1.1516E-19	1.4110E-16	206.216	0
-0.75	0	4.2550E-19	5.6291E-13	408.765	0
-0.5	0	1.8236E-19	1.7707E-13	399.797	0
-0.25	0	1.0415E-19	5.8068E-14	383.707	0
0	0	7.9820E-20	1.9000E-14	359.024	0
0.25	0	7.7654E-20	5.6563E-15	324.685	0
0.5	0	8.9364E-20	1.4238E-15	280.607	0
0.75	0	1.1299E-19	2.8408E-16	227.063	0
-0.5	-0.25	3.5166E-19	1.3293E-13	372.436	0
-0.25	-0.25	1.8645E-19	4.0043E-14	356.042	0
0	-0.25	1.3058E-19	1.1671E-14	330.619	0
0.25	-0.25	1.1922E-19	3.1156E-15	294.959	0
0.5	-0.25	1.3341E-19	6.7641E-16	247.403	0
-0.25	-0.5	3.7376E-19	2.9614E-14	327.124	0
0	-0.5	2.5081E-19	7.9903E-15	300.702	0
0.25	-0.5	2.1853E-19	1.8328E-15	261.999	0
0	-0.75	5.3842E-19	5.3180E-15	266.741	0

Chapter 5

The True Cost-of-Living Concept

5.1   Introduction

This chapter examines the sensitivity of the cost of living to some aspects of price changes and income changes that cannot be detected by Laspeyres indexes such as the CPI-U and CPI-W. Although its content is confined to positive economic analysis, the article does cast light on normative choices in welfare policy. Formation of practical strategies in the negotiation of escalator clauses in private sector wage contracts involves consideration of both normative values and positive descriptions of the real environment. The same is true of policy choices in the political arena, for instance in the determination of cost-of-living adjustments (COLAs) in pensions and transfer payments. The price and income sensitivities of the cost of living, expressed as elasticities, are used to determine the size of COLAs required to keep real incomes of recipients constant.

The sensitivity analysis is applied to a true cost-of-living index (TCLI) that is based on a minimal set of theoretical assumptions; they are just sufficient for its definition to be valid. This use of minimal theory is a safeguard against implicit normative choices that masquerade as positive empirical conclusions.

Private and governmental agencies that prepare and publish cost-of-living indexes have to deal with two distinct kinds of notions of what the term 'true cost-of-living' means:

1. The scientific concept of 'true cost-of-living' as defined by Konyus (1924) and refined by Fisher and Shell (1968). This concept, without extra assumptions, is used to define TCLIs in this chapter.

2. An extra-scientific intuitive conception of 'true cost-of-living' that means something that:

   (a) has an existence in reality independently of the Konyus definition and

   (b) about which the above-mentioned scientific definitions could be empirically "incomplete".[1]

Extra restrictions on (1) are not neutral in their distributional implications. For instance, a TCLI derived on the assumption that consumers' indifference maps are approximately "Leontief", suggests that losses of real income — by (say) a professional couple in Federal employment with GS-15 salaries — since 1972 amounted to about 38%. On the other hand, the minimal assumption TCLI defined in this chapter suggests that the real income loss for GS-15's was only about 8% by 1980. The "Leontief" TCLI, or Laspeyres index, makes a seemingly more persuasive case for raising statutory Federal pay-scales, at upper levels at least, than the minimal assumption TCLI. These percentages are from a research study in progress and are not to be taken as hard and fast (see Basmann, Diamond and Slottje (1988 a,b)). They merely illustrate what we mean by saying that the extra restrictions are not neutral.

TCLIs based on price-dependent preferences (PDP) models involve extra restrictions and lack neutrality, too. Commencing with Samuelson (1948, pp. 119-121), PDP models have arbitrarily ruled out income or total expenditure[2] as affecting cost of living via effects on tastes. The most recent revival of interest in PDP modelling has continued to limit attention

---

[1] Usually because the concept (1) does not impose more than the absolute minimum set of assumptions. For instance, the empirical possibility that the true-cost-of-living be homogeneous of degree one in prices is often conceived to be a necessary condition.

[2] Samuelson introduces a monetary asset, M, into the formal direct utility function, and total expenditure, I, in the budget constraint. Notation in this paper is different. Here in Section 5.2, quantities of monetary assets as well as of goods are denoted by X_i, M denotes total expenditures on goods and monetary assets, and the letter 'I' will be used to denote a cost-of-living index.

to demand systems that arbitrarily exclude some important situations, e.g., Pollak, 1977.

Common sense suggests searching for an index that satisfies the scientific definition (1) of the term 'true cost-of-living' with the absolute minimum of arbitrary assumptions about how consumers' levels of satisfaction depend on the amounts of goods and services they purchase and consume. This minimal set of assumptions is reached by the nonparametric true cost-of-living indexes (TCLIs) based on the generalized Fechner-Thurstone (GFT) form of utility function. The GFT form of direct utility function does not rule out a priori any direct utility function (including any strictly fixed preference direct utility function) that happens to fit empirical data closely, *cf.* Basmann *et al.* (1985a, pp. 75-76). In other words, if the PDP restrictions, or the "Leontief" indifference map hypotheses are approximately true, then this will show up in their likelihood ratio tests nested in the GFT hypothesis.[3]

The sensitivity analysis in this chapter focuses on the positive aspects of questions like the following:

1. Suppose that increases in spendable income alter consumers' tastes, and that this affluence-induced change of taste raises the cost-of-living to consumers. Under what circumstances should this kind of cost-of-living increase be compensated by a COLA?

2. Suppose that commodity price changes and taste changes do take place simultaneously and their combined effect on a cost-of-living index is calculated. It might be an accepted value judgment that the part of the increase in cost of living that is caused solely by the ceteris paribus change of taste should not be compensated by a cost-of-living adjustment (COLA). However, what if at the same time it might be accepted that the part of the increase that is caused solely by the price increases should be fully compensated?

A framework of positive theoretical and empirical analysis is required to separate the former and the latter components of the increase in the cost of living.

Suppose that consumer tastes are affected slightly by price changes. An increase in a cost-of-living index between two periods is the sum of

---

[3]Outcomes of likelihood ratio tests are described in Section 5.5.

three components. The part caused by price increases has two subcomponents. Assuming the value judgment in the preceding paragraph, we have a new normative question to consider. Should the increase in cost of living attributable to the change of tastes induced by the price changes be compensated by a COLA, or not? Once more a framework of positive theoretical and empirical analysis is needed to separate this indirect price effect from the direct substitution effect of price changes on the cost of living.

In this chapter we apply GFT sensitivity analysis to nonparametric TCLIs computed from annual price and expenditure time-series data (1947-1981) provided by Laura Blanciforti of the U.S. Department of Labor.[4] We have aggregated the expenditures and price-indexes for eleven commodity groups into five groups in this chapter. The five groups are:

1. food, beverages and tobacco;

2. clothes, shoes and miscellaneous commodities;

3. housing, energy and utilities;

4. consumer durables and transportation; and

5. medical care, education, recreation, and travel.[5] We shall use 1972 as the base year for the nonparametric TCLIs in this chapter (see Table 5.1).

Section 5.4 describes the minimal set of assumptions about direct utility functions needed to produce numerical measures of the relative cost of living. It also presents the necessary relations subsisting between the price and income elasticities of demand functions and the exponent functions in the GFT direct utility index. Empirical values of the nonparametric TCLIs computed from the Department of Commerce time-series are presented in Table 5.1. All of the theorems and formulas in Section 5.4 are independent of parametric specifications. They are considerably more general than the conditional theorems of PDP models. However, they do not exclude the latter.

---

[4] The price and expenditure data used in this chapter will be sent to readers on request.
[5] 1972 is the base year for the index prices for the commodity groups.

Section 5.5 reintroduces a parametric specification of the GFT direct utility function. This particular parametric specification is only one of many that can be made and tested. Nested within it is a null hypothesis that is observationally equivalent to the CES class of direct utility functions. As a scientific hypothesis about aggregate consumer behavior, the CES class of direct utility functions does not enjoy much empirical support relative to competitors. However, one of the limiting forms of the CES is the Leontief direct utility function. The latter, if it were approximately true, would rationalize the use of a Laspeyres price index, such as the CPI-U or CPI-W, as a true-cost-of-living index. One argument government economists use to support use of the CPI's to schedule COLAs has been that those indexes are "good approximations" to the true-cost-of-living. This widely used claim on behalf of the CPIs is one reason for selecting a GFT parametric specification whose likelihood ratio can be unambiguously appraised relative to that which underlies the reigning CPI's for the CES class.

Table 5.1 Estimates of the True-Cost-of Living Index $TCLI(1)$			
Year	$TCLI(1)$	Year	$TCLI(1)$
1947	0.540	1964	0.761
1948	0.571	1965	0.774
1949	0.566	1966	0.795
1950	0.577	1967	0.814
1951	0.616	1968	0.847
1952	0.627	1969	0.884
1953	0.638	1970	0.925
1954	0.642	1971	0.964
1955	0.647	1972	1.000
1956	0.660	1973	1.050
1957	0.681	1974	1.160
1958	0.695	1975	1.250
1959	0.710	1976	1.320
1960	0.722	1977	1.400
1961	0.729	1978	1.500
1962	0.740	1979	1.650
1963	0.751	1980	1.840
		1981	2.010

$$TCLI(1) = \prod_{i=1}^{n} \frac{p_i^1}{p_i^0}^{\frac{M_i^1}{M_1}}$$

Data utilized here is from the Dept. of Commerce's Bureau of Economic Analysis. Based on the eleven groups used by Blanciforti (1982), we aggregated into five commodity groups. See Data Appendix.

Table 5.2
Index Elasticities for First Order Process (p = 0.7)

Year	$p_1 \frac{\partial}{\partial p_1} \ln I$ (Food)	$p_2 \frac{\partial}{\partial p_2} \ln I$ (Cloth.)	$p_3 \frac{\partial}{\partial p_3} \ln I$ (Housing)	$p_4 \frac{\partial}{\partial p_4} \ln I$ (Dur.)	$p_5 \frac{\partial}{\partial p_5} \ln I$ (Med.)	$p_6 \frac{\partial}{\partial p_6} \ln I$ (Expend.)
1947	0.3331	0.2598	0.1372	0.1687	0.0699	0.0133
1948	0.3185	0.2550	0.1461	0.1763	0.0703	0.0157
1949	0.2942	0.2327	0.1647	0.1891	0.0719	0.0290
1950	0.2730	0.2163	0.1782	0.2071	0.0638	0.0410
1951	0.2908	0.2303	0.1728	0.1924	0.0649	0.0293
1952	0.2951	0.2260	0.1768	0.1853	0.0284	0.0224
1953	0.2766	0.2093	0.1888	0.1947	0.0859	0.0295
1954	0.2780	0.2020	0.1954	0.1891	0.1030	0.0208
1955	0.2598	0.1913	0.1987	0.2054	0.1042	0.0283
1956	0.2573	0.1912	0.2018	0.1971	0.1117	0.0291
1957	0.2555	0.1857	0.2050	0.1964	0.1118	0.0332
1958	0.2630	0.1869	0.2065	0.1844	0.1239	0.0249
1959	0.2459	0.1808	0.2113	0.1933	0.1163	0.0392
1960	0.2427	0.1796	0.2118	0.1913	0.1270	0.0360
1961	0.2434	0.1799	0.2153	0.1823	0.1353	0.0329
1962	0.2337	0.1802	0.2160	0.1886	0.1361	0.0346
1963	0.2285	0.1798	0.2143	0.1932	0.1410	0.0330
1964	0.2262	0.1826	0.2100	0.1954	0.1444	0.0315
1965	0.2263	0.1826	0.2056	0.2014	0.1457	0.0291
1966	0.2309	0.1909	0.1955	0.2018	0.1523	0.0212
1967	0.2247	0.1939	0.1941	0.1998	0.1599	0.0207
1968	0.2230	0.1969	0.1859	0.2065	0.1628	0.0192
1969	0.2247	0.1989	0.1797	0.2060	0.1726	0.0135
1970	0.2330	0.1975	0.1774	0.1987	0.1820	0.0080
1971	0.2220	0.1918	0.1805	0.2078	0.1854	0.0093
1972	0.2229	0.1933	0.1749	0.2078	0.1953	-0.0000
1973	0.2372	0.1977	0.1677	0.2134	0.2011	-0.0158
1974	0.2446	0.1973	0.1741	0.2049	0.1925	-0.0136
1975	0.2445	0.1949	0.1738	0.2026	0.1979	-0.0138
1976	0.2332	0.1861	0.1785	0.2122	0.1992	-0.0091
1977	0.2243	0.1796	0.1817	0.2179	0.2052	-0.0079
1978	0.2272	0.1814	0.1778	0.2179	0.2171	-0.0170
1979	0.2244	0.1739	0.1864	0.2158	0.2098	-0.0090
1980	0.2083	0.1605	0.2090	0.2095	0.1926	0.0153
1981	0.2048	0.1560	0.2112	0.2064	0.2030	0.0142

Table 5.3
Standard Deviations for the Index Elasticities

Year	Food	Clothing	Housing	Durables	Medical	Tot. Expend.
1947	0.111	0.102	0.057	0.096	0.026	0.010
1948	0.110	0.103	0.060	0.099	0.027	0.011
1949	0.109	0.100	0.065	0.104	0.032	0.018
1950	0.110	0.099	0.067	0.112	0.038	0.024
1951	0.110	0.099	0.068	0.106	0.032	0.018
1952	0.107	0.096	0.070	0.101	0.031	0.016
1953	0.106	0.094	0.073	0.105	0.035	0.019
1954	0.103	0.091	0.077	0.102	0.034	0.015
1955	0.102	0.090	0.078	0.110	0.038	0.018
1956	0.101	0.090	0.079	0.106	0.038	0.018
1957	0.100	0.087	0.078	0.104	0.040	0.019
1958	0.098	0.085	0.079	0.098	0.038	0.016
1959	0.098	0.085	0.078	0.101	0.043	0.022
1960	0.096	0.084	0.078	0.100	0.043	0.020
1961	0.095	0.084	0.080	0.096	0.042	0.019
1962	0.094	0.084	0.080	0.099	0.044	0.020
1963	0.092	0.084	0.080	0.101	0.044	0.018
1964	0.092	0.084	0.080	0.103	0.044	0.018
1965	0.092	0.084	0.079	0.106	0.044	0.016
1966	0.091	0.084	0.078	0.105	0.041	0.013
1967	0.089	0.085	0.078	0.105	0.042	0.011
1968	0.088	0.085	0.076	0.108	0.042	0.010
1969	0.086	0.084	0.075	0.107	0.041	0.007
1970	0.086	0.082	0.075	0.103	0.040	0.004
1971	0.085	0.082	0.077	0.108	0.041	0.004
1972	0.083	0.082	0.078	0.111	0.040	0.000
1973	0.085	0.080	0.079	0.111	0.038	0.006
1974	0.086	0.079	0.079	0.106	0.038	0.004
1975	0.086	0.078	0.079	0.105	0.039	0.005
1976	0.085	0.078	0.081	0.110	0.040	0.003
1977	0.084	0.077	0.083	0.114	0.041	0.002
1978	0.083	0.076	0.084	0.113	0.041	0.006
1979	0.085	0.075	0.084	0.112	0.043	0.002
1980	0.086	0.074	0.084	0.110	0.049	0.012
1981	0.085	0.073	0.085	0.108	0.050	0.012

The standard deviation is the square root of the variance. The calculation is discussed in chapter five above.

Section 5.5 also briefly explains a special point about the statistical inference procedures leading up to the maximum likelihood estimates of the price and income elasticities of the nonparametric cost-of-living index.

Table 5.2 contains the price and income elasticities of the nonparametric TCLIs for each year from 1947 to 1981. Although stochastic taste-changers are important, and we give Taylor expansions for TCLI elasticities with respect to stochastic taste-changers — (5.20) — we postpone the publication of numerical values to a later paper.

Table 5.3 presents point estimates of "large-sample" standard deviations of the TCLI elasticity estimates. We do not present the confidence intervals here but give the standard deviations used to construct them.

Table 5.4 presents the maximum likelihood estimates of the sensitivity of marginal rates of substitution to changes in budget constraint parameters. These are inputs to the computation of TCLI elasticities. Table 5.5 gives ranges of the price and income elasticities of the derived demand functions.

Section 5.7 concludes the chapter with a discussion of the significance of the results and some promising lines of future research.

Responding to a suggestion by a colleague, we digress from time to time to contrast the minimal assumptions (GFT) hypotheses with the more restrictive models of price-dependent preferences (PDP). The brevity of our remarks here is due solely to the fact that the mathematical analysis and empirical results in this chapter do not use any results existing in the otherwise highly valuable PDP literature. As mentioned in previous chapters, previous articles have cited the contributions of a number of earlier writers on PDPs, such as Veblen, Scitovsky, Hicks, Samuelson, Kalman, Dusansky, Howitt and Patinkin, Gabor and Granger, and Pollak extensively; *cf.* Basmann *et al.* 1984, 1985a, 1985b.

5.2 Approach and Notation

There are several equally valid procedures for constructing Konus-type TCLI's when preferences between the base and current periods are dissimilar. Each validly constructed index captures a disparate array of taste-change attributes and consequently distinct policy prescription are implied.[6]

While not intended to connote dismay with the remaining alternative procedures the discussion at hand will confine itself to merely two, namely the $TCLI(0)$ and $TCLI(1)$, which are defined below. The approach used in the measure of these indices has been termed the Modified Standard Market Basket (MSB),[7] which employs the notion of cost-of-living as the minimum expenditure that is required to reach the indifference surface, of some direct utility function $V(X;\Upsilon)$, that passes through a specified market basket say X^0 at some specified point in time. Definitional components of the MSB approach include:

1. a unique form $V(X,\Upsilon)$ of direct utility function

2. two distinct values of the parameter vector Υ, Υ^0 and Υ^1

3. and finally a pair of separate price vectors P^0 and P^1.

Since consumer behavior that is constrained by the usual linear budget constraint necessarily results in the maximization of a GFT utility function there will be no loss of generality for the purposes of this section by assuming:

$$V(X,\Upsilon) = U(X;\theta) \tag{5.1}$$

The superscripts 0 and 1 used above denote the distinct parameter and price vectors respectively. Therefore the equation:

$$U(X;\theta^0) = U(X^1;\theta^0) \tag{5.2}$$

implies that the commodity bundle X^1 is contained on the indifference surface when the parameter vector θ^0 is in effect. Similarly the equation:

$$U(X^0;\theta^0) = U(X^0;\theta^1) \tag{5.3}$$

which denotes equality of the utility levels of the indifference surface with parameter θ^0 containing X^0 with the one containing X^0 with parameter θ^1. Figure 5.1 further illustrates this MSB approach: The dashed indifference surface in Figure 5.1 is denoted as $U(X^0;\theta^0)$ which implies the level of

---

[6]See Basmann*et al.* (1985a), Fisher and Shell (1968, pp.97-101) Samuelson and Swamy (1974, pp. 585-586)

[7]See Diamond (1984 p. 25) and Frentrup (1984 p.16)

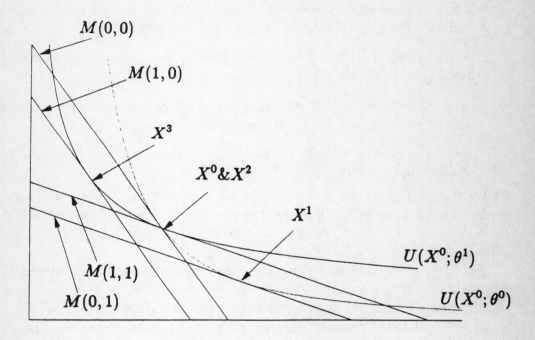

Figure 5.1: The MSB approach to TCLI's

utility which contains the commodity bundle X^0 with parameter vector θ^0.[8] The solid indifference surface denoted as $U(X^0; \theta^1)$, on the other hand, represents the level of utility which contains the same commodity bundle X^0 yet has a different parameter vector, namely θ^1. An explanation of the notation in Figure 5.1 follows:

1. $X^0, \ldots, X^3$ represent various commodity bundles,

2. $M(0,0)$ represents the minimum expenditure required to reach the indifference surface $U(X^0; \theta^0)$ given the price vector P^0,

3. $M(0,1)$ represents the minimum expenditure required to reach the indifference surface $U(X^0; \theta^0)$ given the price vector P^1,

4. $M(1,0)$ represents the minimum expenditure required to reach the indifference surface $U(X^0; \theta^1)$ given the price vector P^0,

5. $M(1,1)$ represents the minimum expenditure required to reach the indifference surface $U(X^0; \theta^1)$ given the price vector P^1.

Under the MSB framework the TCLI's are expressed as ratios of the minimum expenditures given in items 2–5 above. As was mentioned the discussion in this section is limited to the $TCLI(0)$ and $TCLI(1)$, whose definitions follow.

$TCLI(0)$ is the compensating variation required to maintain the original level of utility given the base period parameter vector θ^0 as the price vector changes from the base period (P^0) to the current period (P^1). In other words it is the ratio of the minimum expenditure required to reach the indifference surface $U(X^0; \theta^0)$ given the current price vector P^1 to the minimum expenditure required to reach the identical surface given the base year price vector P^0.

Analogously $TCLI(1)$ is the compensating variation required to maintain the original level of utility given the current parameter vector θ^1 as the price vector changes from the base period (P^0) to the current period (P^1). In other words it is the ratio of the minimum expenditure required to reach the indifference surface $U(X^0; \theta^1)$ given the current price vector P^1 to the minimum expenditure required to reach the identical surface given the base year price vector P^0.

---

[8]the parameter vector θ^a rationalizes the preferences of the individual or group of individuals, when $\theta^a \neq \theta^b$ a change of tastes is implied

5.3 Derivation of the TCLI's

Seo (1973) demonstrated that if γ is constant then there will be no loss in generality by assuming that $\gamma = 0$ which will be done here. However, one would not always assume that the vector γ is constant.[9]

Substituting the demand equation derived from (1.4) back into itself and taking the θth root of both sides of the equation while factoring out the M one obtains the following:

$$[U\,(X;\theta)]^{1/\theta} = \prod_{i=1}^{n} \left(\frac{\theta_i}{\theta}\right)^{\theta_i/\theta} \left(\frac{1}{P_i}\right)^{\theta_i/\theta} M \qquad (5.4)$$

the empirical estimation procedure of θ_i/θ has been demonstrated previously. In equilibrium however we know:

$$P_i X_i^* = \frac{\theta_i}{\theta} M \qquad (5.5)$$

$$P_j X_j^* = \frac{\theta_j}{\theta} M$$

which implies that:

$$\frac{P_i X_i^*}{P_j X_j^*} = \frac{M_i}{M_j} = \frac{\theta_i}{\theta_j} \qquad (5.6)$$

which means that in equilibrium θ_i/θ can be found by expanding (5.6) as follows:

$$\frac{\theta_j}{\theta} = \left[\sum_{i=1}^{n} \frac{\theta_i}{\theta_j}\right]^{-1} \qquad (5.7)$$

$$\frac{\theta_i}{\theta} = \left(\frac{\theta_i}{\theta_j}\right)\left(\frac{\theta_j}{\theta}\right)$$

$$= \frac{M_i}{M}$$

Therefore the TCLI's in this study can either be determined by specifying a functional form or nonparametrically as explained above

---

[9] Notice that this chapter has nothing to do with a test of the Pollak hypothesis that "the snob appeal" effect of prices is confined to the γ_i, $i = 1,\ldots,n$, in (5.13) under the additional assumption that every random disturbance u_i is identically zero, and γ_i remain constant from observation to observation, cf. Pollak (1977, p. 70).

5.3.1   Computation of $TCLI(0)$

Recall that $TCLI(0) = M(0,1)/M(0,0)$ which can alternatively be thought of as the minimum cost of obtaining X^1 relative to the minimum cost of obtaining X^0.[10] The demand equations at X^0 and X^1 appear as:

$$X^0 = \left(\frac{\theta_i^0}{\theta^0}\right)\frac{1}{P_i^0}M(0,0) \tag{5.8}$$

$$X^1 = \left(\frac{\theta_i^0}{\theta^0}\right)\frac{1}{P_i^1}M(0,1)$$

From (5.6) in light of (5.8) it follows:

$$\left[U\left(X^0;\theta^0\right)\right]^{1/\theta^0} = \prod_{i=1}^{n}\left(X_i^0\right)^{\left(\theta_i^0/\theta^0\right)} \tag{5.9}$$

$$= \prod_{i=1}^{n}\left(\frac{\theta_i^0}{\theta^0}\right)^{\left(\theta_i^0/\theta^0\right)}\prod_{i=1}^{n}\frac{1}{P_i^0}^{\left(\theta_i^0/\theta^0\right)}M(0,0)$$

$$\left[U\left(X^1;\theta^0\right)\right]^{1/\theta^0} = \prod_{i=1}^{n}\left(X_i^1\right)^{\left(\theta_i^0/\theta^0\right)}$$

$$= \prod_{i=1}^{n}\left(\frac{\theta_i^0}{\theta^0}\right)^{\left(\theta_i^0/\theta^0\right)}\prod_{i=1}^{n}\frac{1}{P_i^1}^{\left(\theta_i^0/\theta^0\right)}M(0,1)$$

noting that

$$\left[U\left(X^0;\theta^0\right)\right]^{1/\theta^0} = \left[U\left(X^1;\theta^0\right)\right]^{1/\theta^0}$$

it follows that:

$$\prod_{i=1}^{n}\left(\frac{\theta_i^0}{\theta^0}\right)^{\left(\theta_i^0/\theta^0\right)}\prod_{i=1}^{n}\frac{1}{P_i^0}^{\left(\theta_i^0/\theta^0\right)}M(0,0) = \prod_{i=1}^{n}\left(\frac{\theta_i^0}{\theta^0}\right)^{\left(\theta_i^0/\theta^0\right)}\prod_{i=1}^{n}\frac{1}{P_i^1}^{\left(\theta_i^0/\theta^0\right)}M(0,1)$$

$$\tag{5.10}$$

Using (5.12) and the definition of $TCLI(0)$ from above one may obtain the following:

$$TCLI(0) = \frac{M(0,1)}{M(0,0)} = \prod_{i=1}^{n}\left(\frac{P_i^1}{P_i^0}\right)^{\left(\theta_i^0/\theta^0\right)} \tag{5.11}$$

---

[10]refer to Figure 5.11 above

Recall that $TCLI(1) = M(1,1)/M(1,0)$ which can alternatively be thought of as the minimum cost of obtaining X^2 relative to the minimum cost of obtaining X^3.[11] It is easy to show that

$$TCLI(1) = \frac{M(1,1)}{M(1,0)} = \prod_{i=1}^{n} \left(\frac{P_i^1}{P_i^0}\right)^{(\theta_i^1/\theta^1)} \qquad (5.12)$$

5.4   The Sensitivity of the Cost of Living

This section describes the dependencies between sensitivities of nonparametric TCLIs based on the GFT form, and the elasticities of market demand function systems in general. It sets the stage for the specification of statistical hypotheses in Section 5.5. However, the present section is concerned solely with those interdependencies that

1. are true regardless of the parametric specification of demand systems or the direct utility function, and

2. are actually used in the subsequent sections.

The center of interest is the pair of equations (5.17) and (5.18) that relate price and total expenditure elasticities of the cost-of-living to the familiar market price and income elasticities of empirical demand analysis.

The formal principle, or "law" of diminishing marginal rate of substitution between commodities asserts

1. that indifference surfaces are convex, (or, at least, nonconcave) towards the origin of the commodity space, and

2. that the indifference surfaces remain fixed in position over the time period during which the consumer plans and purchases equilibrium quantities of commodities, or obtains them by direct exchange.

For brevity, we call this period a transaction period. Independently of assuming the principle of diminishing marginal rate of substitution, we shall also assume that the consumer selects an equilibrium basket of commodities, X, subject to a linear budget constraint in total expenditure M

---

[11]see Figure 5.1 above

Table 5.4
Coefficient Estimates of the Elasticities of Marginal
Rates of Substitution for Five Commodity Groups
Numeraire = 5

Group	$\omega_{i1}^{(5)}$	$\omega_{i2}^{(5)}$	$\omega_{i3}^{(5)}$	$\omega_{i4}^{(5)}$	$\omega_{i5}^{(5)}$	$\omega_{i0}^{(5)}$
Food:	0.71393 *	0.22090	0.20415	0.03324	-0.9761 *	-0.39580 *
Clothing:	0.21191	0.48245 *	0.18126	-0.15033	-1.1857 *	0.11366
Housing:	0.12729	-0.72948 *	0.93676 *	-0.09344	0.0163	-0.27120
Durables:	-0.79468 *	-0.48543	1.34277 *	-0.08594	-2.4474 *	1.80299 *
Medical:	0.00000	0.00000	0.00000	0.00000	0.00000	0.00000

Note: The asterisks indicate that coefficient estimates were statistically significant at 0.10 level of significance.

and prices p that remains fixed during the transaction period in question. Let M^0 and p^0 denote base period equilibrium demand quantities for this base period. Let p^1 denote the vector of prices in some current period under study. The "law" of diminishing marginal rate of substitution between commodities does not imply that the indifference map in the current period is identical to the indifference map of the base period.

When the indifference maps differ between the base period and the current period, there are several equally valid ways of constructing Konyus-type true-cost-of-living indexes (Fisher and Shell, 1968, pp. 97-101; Samuelson and Swamy, 1974, pp. 585-586; Basmann et al., 1985a, Sec. 2, passim). Each of these validly constructed TCLIs captures effects of a different group of aspects of taste-change. Each of these true-cost-of-living indexes has different policy implications (say) for indexing tax brackets or determining COLAs in pension benefits.

In this chapter, we shall confine our remarks to just two of these valid Konyus type true-cost-of-living index constructions (given in (5.15)-(5.16) below). $TCLI(0)$ is the Konyus index computed from p^0 and p^1 and the base period indifference surface through X^0. $TCLI(1)$ is the Konyus index computed from p^0 and p^1 and the current period indifference surface through X^0. For sake of perspective we mention a Konyus true-cost-of-living index proposed by Fisher and Shell. $TCLI(FS)$ is the Konyus index computed from p^0 and p^1 and the current period equilibrium bundle X^0 (Basmann *et al.*, 1985b, formula (2.9) p. 30). No special form of direct utility function is presupposed by these definitions. For some assumed forms of underlying direct utility unction, $TCLI(1)$ and $TCLI(FS)$ can differ in numerical magnitude. However, under minimal assumptions about the GFT form of direct utility function, the numerical magnitudes of $TCLI(1)$ and $TCLI(FS)$ are identical.

For the time being, we assume only that the consumer (or group of consumers) chooses a market basket subject to the usual linear budget constraint in p and M. Consumer behavior that is constrained by the usual linear budget constraint necessarily results in maximization of a direct utility function having the GFT form.[12] Since the principle of diminishing marginal rate of substitution does not imply that the indifference surfaces are independent of the budget constraint, we shall not make the assumption that they are. The GFT form of direct utility function is recalled as,

$$U(X;\theta) = \prod_{i=1}^{n} (X_i - \gamma_i)^{\theta_i}, \tag{5.13}$$
$$X > \max\{0,\gamma_i\},$$
$$\theta_i = \theta_i^*(p,M,Z)e^{u_i} > 0, \quad i=1,\ldots,n,$$
$$\theta = \sum_{i=1}^{n}\theta_i.$$

$u = (u_1,\ldots,u_n)$ is a latent random vector with zero mean vector and finite positive definitive variance matrix Γ_0. It represents stochastic changes of taste. Serial covariance matrices Γ_s, $s=1,2,\ldots$ may represent persistence of effects of stochastic taste changes, as was discussed in section 5.3.

In empirical applications of the GFT direct utility function $z = (z_1,\ldots,z_r)$ is a vector of observable nonstochastic variables, other than current period p and M, on which consumers' indifference maps may be specified to

---

[12]There are several, more or less, trivial proofs in previous articles: Basmann *et al.* (1983, p. 412); Basmann *et al.* (1985b, p. 20).

Table 5.5
Summary Statistics of the Price Elasticities of Demand

Food	Clothing	Housing	Durables	Medical	Income
$E_{11} < 0$ $(-.45) - (-.34)$ *	$E_{21} > 0$ $(.05) - (.16)$ **	$E_{31} \begin{smallmatrix}<0 & 47-52\\>0 & 53-81\end{smallmatrix}$ $(.03) - (.07)$ **	$E_{41} < 0$ $(-.95) - (-.84)$ **	$E_{51} < 0$ $(-.16) - (-.05)$ **	$E_{10} > 0$ $(.43) - (.35)$ *
$E_{12} > 0$ $(.20) - (.33)$ *	$E_{22} < 0$ $(-.54) - (-.41)$ **	$E_{32} < 0$ $(-.75) - (-.61)$ **	$E_{42} < 0$ $(-.50) - (-.37)$ **	$E_{52} \begin{smallmatrix}<0 & 47-48\\>0 & 49-81\end{smallmatrix}$ $(-.03) - (.10)$ **	$E_{20} > 0$ $(.93) - (.86)$ *
$E_{13} < 0$ $(-.25) - (-.32)$ *	$E_{23} < 0$ $(-.27) - (-.35)$ **	$E_{33} < 0$ $(-.52) - (-.60)$ *	$E_{43} > 0$ $(.88) - (.81)$ **	$E_{53} < 0$ $(-.45) - (-.53)$ *	$E_{30} > 0$ $(.54) - (.48)$ *
$E_{14} > 0$ $(.086) - (.087)$ *	$E_{24} < 0$ $(-.097) - (-.095)$ **	$E_{34} < 0$ $(-.04) - (-.038)$ *	$E_{44} < 0$ $(-1.033) - (-1.031)$ *	$E_{54} > 0$ $(.052) - (.055)$ *	$E_{40} > 0$ $(2.6) - (2.5)$ *
$E_{15} \begin{smallmatrix}>0 & 47-53\\<0 & 53-81\end{smallmatrix}$ $(.05) - (-.07)$ *	$E_{25} < 0$ $(-.15) - (-.28)$ *	$E_{35} > 0$ $(1.05) - (.93)$ *	$E_{45} < 0$ $(-1.21) - (-1.33)$ **	$E_{55} \begin{smallmatrix}>0 & 48-58\\<0 & 58-81\end{smallmatrix}$ $(.03) - (-.09)$ *	$E_{50} > 0$ $(.82) - (.75)$ *

Note:

* indicates no linear time trend is present but values of E 's did decrease slightly over time.

** indicates the same thing as * except the values of E 's increase slightly over time.

- The number in parentheses are the values of E_{is}'s in 1947 and 1981 respectively.

- E_{is}'s < 0 indicates values of E_{is}'s for 1947-1981 are all negative.

- The elasticities are computed from the following relation:

$$E_{is} = S_{is} - \delta_{is} \quad \delta_{is} = 1 \;\; i = s$$

$$\delta_{is} = 0 \;\; i \neq s$$

where

$$S_{is} = \omega_{is}^{(n)} - \sum_{i=1}^{n} \frac{\theta_k}{\theta} \omega_{ks}^{(n)},$$

where n is the numeraire.

depend. Elements of z may be demographic variables, such as family size; they may be lagged values of M or p.

The indifference surfaces of (5.13) satisfy the "law" of diminishing marginal rate of substitution (MRS) at all points X of the commodity space. p, M, and z affect marginal rates of substitution and curvatures of indifference surfaces at every X, but they do not cause violations of the "law" of diminishing MRS. The traditional distinction between arguments and parameters is essential. The vector X of quantities of commodities is the only argument of the GFT direct utility function (5.13). p, M, z, and u are *parameters* of (5.13). Prices are "in the utility function" only in the above sense of that expression. In terms of economic behavior, the argument X is under the consumer group's control, whereas the parameters are not. We assume here that the consumer group does not choose prices and its total expenditure is exogenous. GFT utility functions with several monetary aggregates have been tested and estimated by Johnson (1987, 1988), Pandey (1986) and Opiela (1986).

Every parameter form of system of demand functions $X(p, M; z)$ can be rationalized by a readily constructed parametric case of the GFT direct utility function (Basmann *et al.*, 1983, 1984, 1985a, 1985b). Existence of points p, M, z for which some goods are "inferior" is not ruled out by the form (5.13). In the present article, it is convenient to make use of the close relation between sensitivity of TCLIs and the more familiar concepts of elasticities of demand. [The convenience becomes more apparent in Sec. 5.5.] We do this by showing how to construct the nonrandom parts of (5.13) in terms of demand elasticities directly.[13]

Consider any algorithm for assigning to each sample (p, M, z) in a sample set S logarithmic derivatives of the demand quantities X_i, $i = 1, \dots, n$ with respect to total expenditure M and budget constraint prices, p_j, $j = 1, \dots, n$, and the elements of z. Require the algorithm to produce derivatives that are consistent with the usual budget constraint.[14] These are the only necessary restrictions on the choice of algorithm. In particular there is no reason to force income elasticities to be positive, as in PDP models (Pollak, 1977). Of course, numerical values of the derivatives will depend on the choice of logarithm. However, the relations (5.13) and all

---

[13]This direct approach is often (not always) convenient in constructing (5.13) from previously estimated demand systems such as the translog system.

[14]derivations of the elasticities are given in Basmann and Slottje (1987)

that follow remain valid in spite of differences in the numerical values obtained by different algorithms.

The logarithmic derivatives are elasticities, of course. Let $E_{i0}(p, M, z)$ be demand elasticities with respect to M, and $E_{ij}(p, M, z)$, $i, j = 1, \ldots, n$, be the numerical price elasticities of demand assigned to the observed vector (p, M, z). It is to be expected that these elasticities vary from observation to observation just as they actually do in "real world" per capita time-series data. The positive-valued, nonrandom parts of exponent functions in (5.13), $\theta_i^*(p, M, z)$, are then specified by using $E_{i0}(p, M, z)$ etc. in

$$\theta_i^* = (p_i/M)(\beta_i M^{E_{i0}} \prod_{j=1}^{n} p_j^{E_{ij}})(\prod_{q=1}^{r} z_q^{E_{izq}})K(\cdot)$$

$$\beta_i > 0, \tag{5.14}$$

$$\sum_{i=1}^{n} \beta_i = 1. \quad i = 1, \ldots, n.$$

where

$$K(\cdot) = (\prod_{j=1}^{n} p_j^{c_j})(\prod_{q=1}^{r} z_q^{c_{zq}})M^{c_0}$$

The exponents c_0, c_j, etc. in $K(\cdot)$ are functions of the demand elasticities, E_{i0}, E_{ij}, etc., and commodity expenditure shares (M_i/M), $i = 1, \ldots, n$. They are not necessarily constant. Since $K(\cdot)$ appears as a common factor in (5.14) for each $i = 1, \ldots, n$, its value does not affect the demand functions. Dropping $K(\cdot)$ from (5.13) has the effect of a monotonic increasing transformation of the utility function *cf.* Hicks (1946, pp. 306-307). This does not affect the validity of (5.14).

The GFT direct utility function generates nonparametric true-cost-of-living indexes, thus avoiding the major uncertainties that beset parametric estimation of other forms [for an excellent discussion of these problems see Barnett (1980, 1983) and Barnett and Lee (1985)]. Using (5.13) and (5.14) along with (5.9) above the true-cost-of-living indexes $TCLI(0)$ and $TCLI(1)$ are expressed by the following formulas:

$$\text{GFT--}TCLI(0) = \prod_{i=1}^{n} (\frac{p_i^1}{p_i^0})^{\frac{M_i^0}{M^0}}, \tag{5.15}$$

$$\text{GFT--}TCLI(1) = \prod_{i=1}^{n} (\frac{p_i^1}{p_i^0})^{\frac{M_i^1}{M^1}}, \tag{5.16}$$

M denotes expenditure on the i-th commodity. Superscripts indicate the period in which the expenditure is made.

A very brief remark about (5.15)-(5.16) may be helpful. In deriving (5.15)-(5.16), the expression θ_i/θ — with appropriate superscripts — is first encountered where the ratio M_i/M appears in (5.15)-(5.16). The ratio θ_i/θ is the proportionate marginal utility of income expended on the i-th commodity. At equilibrium the proportionate marginal utility of income expended on the i-th commodity necessarily equals the equilibrium expenditure share M_i/M as was shown in (5.9) above. This is true regardless of the form of direct utility function. Consequently, it is not necessary to estimate the ratio θ_i/θ where it is assumed that sample expenditures are equilibrium magnitudes, since — apart from errors of measurement in the data themselves — θ_i/θ is known exactly.

Table 5.1 presents the values of $TCLI(1)$, i.e., (5.16) for the years 1947-81 in the United States.

Let $E_{is}(p, M; z)$ be the elasticity of demand for the i-th commodity with respect to the budget constraint price p_s. [Let us abbreviate this function by E_{is}.] The GFT form of direct utility function expresses the sensitivity of the cost of living to price changes in terms of the demand elasticities E_{ij} in a straightforward way (recall 5.13). The elasticity of the nonparametric GFT-$TCLI(1)$ with respect to the price p_s is expressed by the formula

$$(p_s \frac{\partial}{\partial p_s}) \ln I = \sum_{i=1}^{n} \frac{\theta_i}{\theta} \left[E_{is} \ln \left(\frac{p_i}{p_i^0} \right) \right] + \frac{\theta_s}{\theta} \left[1 + \ln \left(\frac{p_s}{p_s^0} \right) \right], \qquad (5.17)$$

$$s = 1, 2, \ldots, n.$$

The superscript "1" has been dropped; the superscript "0" has been kept in order to indicate that p is a constant for the differentiation of (5.16). Derivation of (5.18) is given in Basmann and Slottje (1987).

The elasticity (5.17) is nonparametric. That is to say, its numerical magnitude does not depend on the parametric forms of the proportionate marginal utilities of expenditure θ_i/θ. Notice that the demand elasticities in (5.17) do not presuppose any special parametric form of demand function system.

The part of the proportional increase in cost of living that is attributable to a specified price-induced change of taste is essentially a weighted average of price elasticities of demand. This is one practical

convenience in constructing (5.13) in terms of demand function elasticities directly. If (for instance) it is a normative consensus that cost of
living increases caused by changes of taste should not be compensated by
COLAs, then it is an advantage that every concept involved in measuring
the not-to-be-compensated part is already well understood.

The income elasticity of the GFT form of $TCLI(1)$ is expressed by the
following formula:

$$(M\frac{\partial}{\partial M}) \ln I = \sum_{i=1}^{n} \frac{\theta_i}{\theta} [E_{is} - 1] \ln \left(\frac{p_i}{p_i^0}\right), \tag{5.18}$$

Derivation of (5.18) is given in Basmann and Slottje (1987).

The sensitivities of $TCLI(1)$ with respect to other systematic taste
changers in z are expressed by formulas similar to (5.18). However, no
systematic taste changers other than p and M will be used in the application to follow, so we omit expressions for their elasticities.

The sensitivity of $TCLI(1)$ with respect to the stochastic taste changer
u_j is expressed by

$$u_j \frac{\partial}{\partial u_j} \ln I = u_j \sum_{i=1}^{n} \left[\ln \frac{p_i^1}{p_i^0}\right] \frac{\partial}{\partial u_j} \varsigma_i, \tag{5.19}$$

$$j = 1, \ldots, n,$$

where the derivative of ς_i is expressed by its Taylor expansion[15]

$$\frac{\partial}{\partial u_j} \varsigma_i = \frac{\theta_i^*}{\theta^*} \left(\delta_{ji} - \frac{\theta_j^*}{\theta^*}\right) + \left[\sum_{m=2}^{r} \left(\frac{D^{m-1}}{(m-1)!}\right)(\delta_{ji} - \lambda_j)\lambda_i \right.$$

$$\left. + \frac{D^r}{(r+1)!} (r + \tau D) \left(\delta_{ji} - \lambda_j^*\right) \lambda_i^* \right]_{w=0} \tag{5.20}$$

where D is the linear differential operator $\frac{\partial}{\partial u_j}$ and

$$\lambda_j = \frac{\theta_j(p_i, M, Z)e^{w_i}}{\sum_{k=1}^{n} \theta_k^*(p, M, z)e^{w_k}} \tag{5.21}$$

and

$$\lambda_j^* = \lambda(p, M, z, w + \tau u). \tag{5.22}$$

---

[15] ς is the random disturbance in the jth expenditure share, M_j/M. The derivation of
(5.19) is given in the article by Basmann et al. (1985a), pp. 73-75.

It is by no means certain just how many terms of the Taylor expansion (5.19) are required to get a prescribed closeness of approximation, $e > 0$, or how small e should be in this kind of application. We face the same problem here as with the Taylor expansions of (5.17) and (5.18) used in computing the "large sample" standard deviations in Table 5.3. In the latter computations discarding all but the linear terms, as described in Kmenta (1971, p. 444; see also Zellner *et al.*, 1965) is not unusual in practice. However, it is easy to be misled since reliability of that approach is far from uniform over the range of its applications.

The chief practical use of the index elasticities (5.17) and (5.18) is in determining the increase of nominal expenditure, M, just required to compensate the loss of real income due to a given increase in the price p of some commodity s. The economic concept of real expenditure is dependent on the form of indifference map and involves using the TCLI derived from that form as a deflator of nominal total expenditure. For instance, use of the CPI-U as a deflator presupposes that the indifference map is approximately of the "Leontief" form. The GFT-real expenditure, denoted here by U^*, is total expenditure M deflated by GFT-$TCLI(1)$:

$$U^* = \frac{M}{TCLI(1)}, \tag{5.23}$$

$$= \frac{M}{\prod_{i=1}^{n} \left(p_i/p_i^0\right)^{\frac{\theta_i}{\theta}}}$$

Setting the total derivative of (5.23) equal to zero and solving, one obtains

$$\frac{p_s}{M}\frac{\partial M}{\partial p_s} = \frac{p_s \frac{\partial}{\partial p_s}\ln I}{1 - M\frac{\partial}{\partial M}\ln I} \tag{5.24}$$

This is the proportionate change of nominal expenditure M required to compensate a one percent increase in the price p_s to hold real expenditure constant.

In the next section two additional relations are used in the specification of a maintained statistical hypothesis. These relate elasticities of marginal rates of substitution to elasticities of demand functions. We use $\omega_{i0}^{(n)}$, $\omega_{is}^{(n)}$ $s = 1, \ldots, n$, to denote the elasticity of the MRS of commodity n for commodity i with respect to total expenditure, M, and p_s, respectively. The choice of numeraire, commodity n, is arbitrary. For $i = n$, the elasticities denoted above are identically 0.

Elasticities of demand with respect to price and with respect to total expenditure are related to MRS elasticities by the following equations:

$$E_{is} = \omega_{is}^{(n)} - \sum_{k=1}^{n} \frac{\theta_k}{\theta} \omega_{ks}^{(n)} - \delta_{is}, \tag{5.25}$$

$$E_{i0} = \omega_{i0}^{(n)} - \sum_{k=1}^{n} \frac{\theta_k}{\theta} \omega_{k0}^{(n)} + 1 \quad i, s = 1, \ldots, n.$$

where $\delta_{ii} = 1$; if $s \neq i$, then $\delta_{is} = 0$. Inverse relations are found in Basmann and Slottje (1987).

The validity of (5.21) is independent of the parametric specifications of (5.13).

5.5   Statistical Methods used in the Chapter

In this chapter the statistical estimates of price and income elasticities of the GFT-$TCLI(1)$ presented in Table 5.2 are obtained by substituting observed prices p, expenditure shares, $\frac{M_i}{M}$, $i = 1, \ldots, n$, and maximum likelihood estimates $\hat{\omega}_{ks}^{(n)}, \omega_{k0}^{(n)}$ into the following formulas:

$$p_s \frac{\partial}{\partial p_s} \ln I = \sum_{i=1}^{n} \frac{\theta_i}{\theta} \left[\omega_{is}^{(n)} - \sum_{k=1}^{n} \frac{\theta_k}{\theta} \omega_{ks}^{(n)} \right] \ln \frac{p_i}{p_i^0} + \frac{\theta_s}{\theta} \tag{5.26}$$

$$s = 1, \ldots, n;$$

$$M \frac{\partial}{\partial M} \ln I = \sum_{i=1}^{n} \frac{\theta_i}{\theta} \left[\omega_{i0}^{(n)} - \sum_{k=1}^{n} \frac{\theta_k}{\theta} \omega_{k0}^{(n)} \right] \ln \frac{p_i}{p_i^0}. \tag{5.27}$$

We include complete derivations of (5.26) and (5.27) in the Appendix to Basmann and Slottje (1987).

Maximum likelihood methods necessitate the complete specification of a parent population sample density function. Even if (5.13) is augmented by the hypothesis that the random vector u is normally distributed, it is not practicable to treat the whole class of parent populations as a grand maintained hypothesis. Our practice has been to tackle subclasses of the whole GFT class sequentially. Initially our study has focused on the two maintained hypotheses that permit likelihood ratio tests of the more popular forms of strict neoclassical utility functions:

1. the CES (constant elasticity of substitution) direct utility function, and

2. the CRES (constant ratio of elasticities of substitution) direct utility function.[16]

In this chapter the sole purpose[17] for likelihood ratio tests of strict neoclassical direct utility functions as null hypotheses is to guard against implicit normative judgments; see remarks in Sec. 5.1. If a sample of data gives strong likelihood ratio support (Edwards, 1972, ch. 3 esp. pp. 30-32) to a strictly neoclassical direct utility function, then it gives essentially equal support to at least two distinct TCLIs; *cf.* Basmann *et al.* (1985a, 1985b). To ignore (say) the TCLI based on the strictly neoclassical direct utility function, and confine attention to the nonparametric TCLI would be to make a normative choice by default. Different TCLIs call for different timing and amounts of COLAs and, consequently, different redistributions of welfare.

The GFT-CEMRS (constant elasticity of marginal rates of substitution) is the maintained hypothesis within which the CES direct utility function and its popular limiting forms, "Cobb-Douglas" and "Leontief", can be subjected to likelihood ratio evaluation. The statistical estimates of the index elasticities in Table 5.2 are based on unconstrained ML estimates of the constant MRS elasticities $\hat{\omega}_{ks}^{(n)}, \hat{\omega}_{k0}^{(n)}$ that appear in (5.26). The GFT-CEMRS maintained hypothesis is specified in the multivariate general linear hypothesis form

$$\ln \frac{M_i}{M_n} = \ln \frac{\beta_i}{\beta_n} + \omega_{i0}^{(n)} \ln M + \sum_{j=1}^{n} \omega_{ij}^{(n)} \ln p_j + \eta_i^{(n)}, \qquad (5.28)$$

$$\eta_i^{(n)} = u_i - u_n; \quad i = 1, 2, \ldots, n - 1.$$

---

[16]The formal properties of the CRES form have been studied by Mukerji (1963, p. 233), Gorman (1965), Hanoch (1971, pp. 708-711; 1975, pp. 416-418) and Barnett (1981), pp. 265-266). The CES form is a special case of CRES. For the GFT direct utility function yielding the Leser-Houthakker "addilog" demand function systems, see Basmann *et al.* (1985a, pp. 51-52).

[17]In this study, the GFT utility function (5.13) is applied to the percapita expenditure and demand system for a group of consumers. There is no theoretical basis for expecting its derived demand systems to possess the properties of zero homogeneity, symmetry and negative semi-definiteness of substitution terms; *cf.* Schultz (1938, pp. 628-633). Testing whether the percapita demands are those of an "ideal" consumer is not relevant here.

ML estimators of coefficients and variance matrix $Q^{(n)}$ are obtained by grid search over a family of autoregressive models of the random disturbances in (5.28), a distinct estimate being obtained for each specification in that family. The behavioral theory of random taste-changers underlying the specification of serial correlation hypotheses is given in a recent article (Basmann, 1985). Only two of the assumptions of that theory (Basmann, 1985, pp. 199-202) were used in obtaining the estimates shown in Tables 5.2, 5.3, 5.4 and 5.5 here. They imply that the random disturbances $\eta_i^{(n)}$ $i = 1, \ldots, n - 1$. follow the same first-order autoregressive process. Consequently, the grid search for ML test statistics and estimators is over the interval $-1 < \rho < 1$.

Iterative SUR (seemingly unrelated regression) methods (Zellner, 1962) are used where null hypotheses, such as CES and its limiting forms, and "addilog" direct utility functions, imply cross-equation restrictions[18] on (5.27).

The overriding reason for calculating the index elasticities (5.26) from unconstrained ML coefficient estimates in (5.27) is that the Department of Commerce price and expenditure data (1947-81) afford the popular strict neoclassical utility functions almost no support in likelihood ratio tests. We mention some typical cases from chapter 5. The CES direct utility function, its limiting "Cobb-Douglas" and "Leontief" forms, and the Leser-Houthakker "addilog" form, when tested as null hypotheses within the CEMRS class, yield very large test criteria[19] with negligible probabilities of occurrence under the null hypothesis; these probabilities are $= 0.001e-20$.

The CRES direct utility function cannot be tested within the GFT-CEMRS class because it implies that the MRS elasticities in (5.28) are not constant, but vary linearly with the demand elasticities E_{is} and E_{i0}, and in strongly restricted form. Department of Commerce time-series used in this study give almost no support to the CRES direct utility function. In a recent test, the most favorable[20] test criterion $-2 \ln \lambda$, with 15 degrees of freedom, was 44.9, and the associated probability is 0.00011 under the CRES hypothesis.

Outcomes of likelihood ratio tests of GFT direct utility functions that

---

[18]Including zero coefficient specifications.

[19]*I.e.*, $-2 \ln \lambda$, where λ is the maximum ratio of the likelihood of null hypothesis to likelihood of maintained hypothesis obtained over the ρ grid.

[20]*I. e.*, over the ρ grid.

rationalize flexible demand system forms, such as the translog (Christensen *et al.*, 1975), the Fourier flexible form (Gallant, 1981), or the minflex Laurent (Barnett, 1983; Barnett, 1985; Barnett *et al.*, 1985) might turn out to be favorable. However, we have not made such tests thus far. The larger number of parameters to be estimated relative to the sample size ($n = 33$) would require use of auxiliary restrictions, at least if the present five-commodity aggregation were to be retained.

5.6   The Empirical Results

Table 5.2 is the focal point of this section. It contains the maximum likelihood estimates of GFT-$TCLI(1)$ elasticities with respect to market prices and per capita total expenditure on commodities. However, these elasticities can be most effectively analyzed only in the context of their necessary relations with the MRS elasticities of the GFT direct utility function (5.13) and the price and income elasticities E_{ij}, E_{i0}, of per capita market demand functions. Demand analysts have accumulated considerable experience with empirical elasticities of market demand functions. The existence of "expert" intuitions about plausible magnitudes for market demand elasticities provides the chief motive for writing the nonrandom part of the GFT direct utility function exponents, (5.13), in terms of the familiar market demand elasticities.

Plausible value-ranges for market demand elasticities readily produce corresponding plausible value-ranges for the MRS elasticities. Relations found in Basmann and Slottje (1987) Appendix B, show that MRS elasticities $\omega_{i0}^{(n)}$ and $\omega_{ij}^{(n)}$ are (essentially) the differences between demand function elasticities.

From a formal point of view, it is immaterial where we start the discussion of results. The index elasticities defined in (5.17), (5.18), and (5.26) make that clear. However, it is convenient here to start with estimates of the MRS elasticities, chiefly because the latter are constants in the CEMRS class of GFT utility functions specified as the maintained statistical hypothesis in Sec. 5.5. From those estimates we can compute estimates of the demand function elasticities, E_{i0}, E_{ij} and examine them for possible anomalous values. This is important because likelihood ratio tests of the constancy of the MRS elasticities cannot be performed

within the CEMRS class itself. Demand elasticity estimates greatly out
of line with those in other empirical demand studies would signal a need
for special caution.

Maximum likelihood estimates of the MRS elasticities are given in
Table 5.4. A suitable of MRS elasticity estimates is given for each of the
five ways of specifying the numeraire, n. The five matrices of elasticities
are functionally dependent: given any one them, the remaining four can
be obtained by a simple transformation of the matrix initially specified.
The transformation is

$$\omega_{i0}^{(k)} = \omega_{i0}^{(n)} - \omega_{k0}^{(n)},$$

$$\omega_{ij}^{(k)} = \omega_{ij}^{(n)} - \omega_{kj}^{(n)}, \quad i,j,k = 1,\ldots,n. \tag{5.29}$$

The statistical estimates in Table 5.4 are data of the kind out of which
opinions based on "expert" intuitions concerning plausible values of market demand elasticities can be sharpened. For that reason chiefly[21] we
present the MRS elasticity estimates for each numeraire specification. The
point estimates are augmented by their interval estimates $(1 - \alpha = 0.9)$.
Own-price MRS elasticities that are significantly greater than $+1$ are especially interesting because their existence is a necessary condition (not
sufficient, however) for occurrence of positive own-price elasticities of demand functions. Such exceptions to the Law of Demand reverse the normal own-price effect on the cost-of-living, which is negative, as shown by
(5.17).

The CEMRS specification does not result in anomalous estimates of
demand function elasticities. Ranges of the latter are shown in Table
5.6. [However, the coincidence of a positive own-price elasticity E_{55} and
positive income elasticity E_{50} (medical care, etc., 1948-58 is seemingly
anomalous only from a strictly neoclassical, microtheoretical extrapola-
tion.]

(5.13) implies that a necessary and sufficient condition for a positive
own-price elasticity of demand is that the expenditure-share weighted average of own-price MRS elasticities (over all numeraire specifications) be
greater than $+1$. This happened in the case of commodity 5, the medical

---

[21]Formulas (5.21) and (5.26) do make clear that only one numeraire specification is
required for the computation of maximum likelihood estimates of demand function elasticities and index elasticities.

care group, for the years 1948-58. The medical care group was the only commodity having any own-price MRS elasticity that was significantly greater than +1; see Table 5.4, numeraire specifications 2 (clothing and miscellaneous) and 4 (durables). For numeraire specification 3 (housing services) the medical care own-price MRS elasticity is zero. Downward trends in the expenditure shares for durables, clothing, food, and the upward trend in the expenditure share on housing, account for the return of negative own-price elasticity of medical care since 1958.

Table 5.5 shows that with only two exceptions all price elasticities of demand were less than 1 in absolute value for every year 1947-1981. Demand for durables (commodity group 4) appears to be just elastic, with E_{44} never much smaller than -1. This is the only own-price demand elasticity whose maximum likelihood estimates, while negative, are not considerably larger than -1.

With one exception per capita demand functions are inelastic with respect to total expenditure. The exception is the demand for durables (commodity 4). The maximum likelihood estimates of E_{40} are considerably larger than +1. This is easily traceable to the magnitudes of the MRS elasticities of durables with respect to per capita total expenditure. These are shown in the right-most column of Table 5.4.

We turn to the results summarized in Table 5.2. The point estimates of TCLI-elasticities are direct functions of the maximum likelihood point estimates of MRS-elasticities in Table 5.4. The latter are normally distributed and validity of the use of Student's t-statistics in construction of interval estimates is not problematical. However, in the case of the TCLI elasticities (5.26), the normally distributed estimates of MRS elasticities are multiplied by products of ratios of linear functions of lognormal variables. Little is known about their statistical distribution functions, and there is no expert knowledge about how large a sample must be in order to warrant their "large sample" approximation by a normal distribution. Still it will be useful to provide some tentative "large sample" standard deviations along with the point estimates of TCLI elasticities.

The assessment of contributions of income-induced and price-induced taste changes to changes in GFT-$TCLI(1)$ which follows is internal to the GFT direct utility function. Comparisons of corresponding elasticities of two or more TCLI's based on different utility functions would be superfluous or irrelevant to likelihood testing of one against the others.

For instance the Leontief form of utility function was rejected against the CEMRS with a significance probability < 0.0001 (*cf.* chapter four); however, the price-elasticities of the corresponding TCLI's are very nearly the same for some commodity groups. TCLI elasticities with respect to durable-services price and medical services price were considerably different. The irrelevance to statistical testing of alternative utility functions and TCLIs does not mean that such comparisons would be uninteresting (Edwards, 1972, pp. 30-31).

Analysis of the cost-of-living index elasticities in Table 5.2 indicates that the contribution of price-induced taste changes is substantial, at least for the prices of several commodity groups. By 'substantial' we mean that if the index were to be "corrected" in the legislation of COLA payment schedules, then the resulting effects on timing and size of COLAs, and their cumulated effects over time, would create a significant redistribution of welfare, transfers, etc.[22] The part of a GFT-$TCLI(1)$ elasticity with respect to p_s that is due to price-induced changes of tastes[23] is expressed by the first right-hand term (summation) in (5.26). We review some typical cases computed from Table 5.2.

The share of a $TCLI(1)$ elasticity contributed by such taste changes is not constant and may be quite large. We start by examining the first and last years in our time-series. In 1947 the taste change contributions to $TCLI(1)$ elasticities were

1. +2.5% for food;

2. +4.9% for clothing;

3. +12.78% for housing;

4. -2.4% for durables; and

5. -95.45% for medical care, etc.

In 1981, price-induced changes of taste contributed

1. -3.7% for food;

---

[22]In other words, the resulting distribution would be significantly different from the distribution of welfare under the "uncorrected" COLA schedule.

[23]*I.e.*, changes in marginal rates of substitution that are induced by the change in p_s.

2. -9.7% for clothing;

3. +7.8% for housing;

4. +.4% for durables; and

5. -6.1% for medical care, etc.

Larger taste change contributions to $TCLI(1)$ price elasticities occur in other years. For instance, in 1950 price-induced taste change contributed about -114.6% of the cost-of-living elasticity with respect to the price of medical care; and it contributed +22.9% to the cost-of-living elasticity with respect to the price of housing. Medical care price-induced taste changes counteract increases in the cost-of-living index, typical contributions being -39.7% (1955), -29.9% (1960). -21.1% (1965), declining — in absolute magnitude — more or less steadily to -6.1% in 1981. Taste changes induced by variations of the price of housing augment increases in the $TCLI(1)$, typical contributions being +18.6% (1955), +17.3% (1960), +13.82% (1965), etc.

Taste changes induced by variations in the price of durables generally counteract increases in the $TCLI(1)$, but the contributions are small. Price-induced taste change contributed about -8.6% to the $TCLI(1)$ elasticity with respect to the price of food in 1960; in 1965 the contribution was about -7.5%.

In chapter 4, we presented likelihood ratio tests of the two extreme limiting forms of the CES direct utility function, i.e. Leontief, and "Cobb-Douglas". Since those forms were more or less decisively rejected against the GFT-CEMRS form of (5.13), there was no expectation that the $TCLI(1)$ would be exactly homogeneous of degree 1 in prices. However, the sum of the $TCLI(1)$ price elasticities tends to be very near to 1, varying from about 0.97 to 1.02.

$TCLI(1)$ elasticities with respect to per capita total expenditure appear in the right-most column of Table 5.2. Formula (5.26) shows that the GFT direct utility function (5.13) attributes the whole elasticity to total expenditure induced changes of taste ('M-induced' for short). The cost-of-living is readily seen to have been inelastic with respect to M (given the time-series of annual average prices).[24] The significantly small magnitudes of the $TCLI(1)$ elasticities with respect to M were to be expected from the outcome of the likelihood ratio tests mentioned in Section 5.5. Although (5.13) includes a subclass of homothetic utility functions, the likelihood ratio test rejected homotheticity more or less decisively.

Since the likelihood ratio tests decisively rejected all strictly neoclassical utility functions nested in the GFT-CEMRS maintained hypothesis, it was not expected that the cost-of-living would be homogeneous of degree zero in prices and expenditure, i. e., that the sum of $TCLI(1)$ elasticities would be approximately zero.

Table 5.3 presents "large sample" standard deviations of the estimated elasticities of $TCLI(1)$. The procedure is described in Kmenta (1971, p. 44). One considers (5.26) as a function of the MRS-elasticities, forms the Taylor-Maclaurin expansion around the parameter point, drops all second- and higher-order terms of the expression, takes expectations of the squared linear terms, and substitutes parameter estimates in the resulting variance expression. Lower and upper terminals of the corresponding 90% confidence intervals are given in Basmann and Slottje (1987).

If the assumptions on which these 90% confidence intervals are not too inaccurate, then the directions of the income-induced taste change effects on $TCLI(1)$, indicated by the point estimates, are made somewhat less uncertain. These confidence intervals make interesting the comparison of the $TCLI(1)$ with the corresponding CPI, chiefly because the income-elasticity of the CPI is forced to zero a priori. If the GFT direct utility function underlying the $TCLI(1)$ were near (in parameter space) to its limiting Leontief form, which rationalizes the CPI, then the failure of 90% confidence intervals to include zero would be surprising. On the other hand, the actual result is a "surprise" to the claim that the CPI price indexes are good approximations to the true-cost-of-living.

In Table 5.2 each of the 165 point estimates of $TCLI(1)$ elasticities with respect to price is accompanied by a "large sample" estimate of its standard deviation in Table 5.3. The latter is obtained from (5.26) by the procedure outlined in the preceding paragraph. The ten "large sample" covariances that correspond to each of the point estimates of $TCLI(1)$ elasticities in Table 5.2 are necessary in the construction of "large sample"

---

[24]These elasticities are significant only near the base year (1972) where that is to be expected on analytic grounds.

confidence regions. The "large sample" covariances are obtained in the same manner as the "large sample" variances. Inversion of the "large sample" variance submatrix corresponding to prices determines the axes of the 5-dimensional ellipsoid forming the "large sample" confidence region for price-induced taste-changes affecting $TCLI(1)$. We take for granted the reader's knowledge and experience with the use of confidence region tests of simple hypotheses, such as the null hypothesis that the price-induced taste change components of $TCLI(1)$ price elasticities are all equal to zero, and with the chief limitations of such tests.

Of course, the CEMRS subclass of GFT direct utility functions specified by (5.28) does not exclude the hypothesis that price-induced taste change components of $TCLI(1)$ price elasticities (5.26) are small relative to the effects of the stochastic taste changers. Consequently, the simple hypothesis just described is an important one. Suppose that the outcome of the confidence region test is favorable[25] to the hypothesis that price-induced taste change effects on (5.26) are zero. Then the natural next step is to inquire more deeply into the theory of serially correlated stochastic taste changers (Basmann, 1985, esp. 196-203). Broadly speaking, this is a theory of stochastic habit persistence and habit extinction.

Naturally there are other motivations, some which may not occur to us, but to the readers. The GFT approach to the analysis of demand by aggregates of consumers affords another motivation for testing the hypothesis just mentioned. Basmann et al (1985a, pp. 17-18) describes some "ad hoc theory" relevant to the interpretation of confidence intervals for the price-elasticities of the $TCLI(1)$ based on the GFT direct utility function. The GFT explanation for the rarity of exceptions to the "law of demand" is that operative budget constraint prices exert small, but not universally negligible effects on consumers' indifference maps. This leads to the expectation that taste-change effects on $TCLI(1)$ may require several years' accumulation in a single direction to become significant.

The negative $TCLI(1)$ elasticity with respect to the price of medical care is accounted for in part by results in Table 5.3 (numeraire 5). The elasticities of marginal rate of substitution of medical care for food, clothing, and durables services are all significantly negative and elastic. The elasticity of marginal rate of substitution of medical care for hous-

---

[25]At a prescribed level of significance for the decision in question.

ing, though positive, is very small. Moreover, the exact finite sample test statistics, t, is 0.0676, df = 28. On the hypothesis that $\omega_{35}^{(5)} = 0$, the significance probability of the outcome is 0.947.

The estimated marginal rate of substitution of medical care for durables is very negative-elastic, the next-to-largest in Table 5.4. The marginal rate of substitution of housing for durables is not significantly larger, however. Table 5.4 shows that the marginal rates of substitution of durables services for any numeraire is statistically significantly negative and elastic. This leads to the conjecture that –in the aggregate– a ceteris paribus increase in the price of medical care tends to reduce consumers' valuation of durables services relative to the other commodities. With price changes sufficiently larger, the reduced consumption of durable services is sufficient to offset the effect of the increase in price on the $TCLI(1)$.

5.7   Chapter Summary

Effects of price- and income-induced changes in consumer tastes on the cost of living in the United States from 1947-1981 have been estimated and found to be generally substantial. Up to the mid-1970s income-induced changes of taste tended to increase the cost of living ceteris paribus, failing to offset the inflationary effects of a steady and general increase of prices. After that the effect of income-induced changes of taste has been to decrease the cost of living.

Likelihood ratio tests and maximum likelihood estimation of parameters composed the methods of statistical inference used in the study. Section 5.1 showed how these and similar estimates can assist in the making of normative, welfare policy choices, and how such use calls for the use of TCLIs based on a minimal set of assumptions about consumers' maximizing behavior.

There are several directions in which further research is promising. The estimation of effects of price- and income-induced taste changes on cost of living can be applied to a variety of different data sets, groupings of commodities into composite commodities, the price and expenditure data from different countries.

Estimation of effects of price- and income-induced changes in consumer tastes on the cost of living with variable MRS elasticities and demand elasticities linearly dependent[26] will serve as alternative estimates about equally well-supported as the CEMRS based estimates presented in Table 5.2. Plans also have been made for using the translog subclass of (5.13) as a maintained hypothesis for the estimation of price- and income-induced effects on cost of living.[27]

---

[26]Mentioned in Sec. 5.5. This is the GFT class within which the CRES direct utility function was tested.

[27]See Johnson (1987,1988)

Chapter 6

Cross Country Comparisons

6.1 Introduction

In a recent paper, Hayes, Molina and Slottje (1988) examined the question of preference variation across North America. As the economy of the United States becomes a more open economy and less immune to fluctuations in international markets, the impact of relative price changes of foreign commodities on domestic economic well-being will be of increasing interest. Earlier studies have focused on the welfare impact of foreign price changes (*cf.* Thursby (1981)). In this chapter, potential secondary utility effects of foreign prices are examined, the chapter follows Hayes, Molina and Slottje (1988).

6.2 The Model

The general form of the Fechner-Thurstone direct utility function (Thurstone, 1931, p. 142, p. 147; also Schultz, 1938, p. 15) we utilize is:

$$U(X; P, M, \epsilon) = \prod_{i=1}^{n} (X_i - \gamma_i)^{\beta_i M^{\sigma_{i0}} \prod_{k=1}^{n} p_k^{\sigma_{ik}} \prod_{\ell=1}^{m} z_\ell^{\sigma_{i\ell} \epsilon_i}} \tag{6.1}$$

where $\beta > 0$ and $X_i \geq \max(0, \gamma_i)$. The Z vector represents additional preference changing parameters (besides prices and income).[1] Here Z is

---

[1] The notion of price-dependent preferences is used here but any parameter that affects preferences within and between countries could be discussed in this general framework

defined as the ratio of a foreign price index (deflated by the exchange rate) to the domestic price index. The elasticities of the M.R.S., with respect to a change in α_j in (6.1) are in general:

$$\omega_{i,\alpha_j}^{(k)} = \frac{\alpha_j}{R_i^{(k)}} \frac{\partial R_i^{(k)}}{\partial \alpha_j} = \frac{\alpha_j}{U_i} \frac{\partial U_i}{\partial \alpha_j} - \frac{\alpha_j}{U_k} \frac{\partial U_k}{\partial \alpha_j} \tag{6.2}$$

as we noted in chapter three.

For this chapter we focus on three variables which may have an impact on the MRS and thereby indicate Veblen effects. The first variable is relative prices. If a change in the price of the ith good has an effect on the marginal rate of substitution between any two goods, the elasticity of the MRS with respect to that price will not be zero. This would tell us that the price change caused a change in preferences. In this case, $\alpha_k = p_j$ and (6.2) becomes, as we have seen before,

$$\omega_{i,p_j}^{(k)} = \sigma_{ij} - \sigma_{kj} \tag{6.3}$$

Secondly, we are concerned with the impact of a change in M on the MRS. If a change in total expenditures causes a change in the MRS, then we can conclude that a change in M changes the preference structure. In terms of (6.2), $\alpha_k = M$ and

$$\omega_{i,M}^{(k)} = \sigma_{i0} - \sigma_{k0} \tag{6.4}$$

Finally, we also focus on foreign price effects. If the MRS changes as a result of a change in relative foreign prices, this indicates a shift in preferences in response to the foreign price change. In this case, $\alpha_k = Z_\ell$ and

$$\omega_{i,Z_\ell}^{(k)} = \tilde{\sigma}_{i\ell} - \tilde{\sigma}_{k\ell} \tag{6.5}$$

The unknown σ_{i,p_j}'s are assumed to be independent of market prices p_k, $k \neq j$, total expenditure, M, and Z_ℓ. The σ_{i0} are assumed to be independent of market prices p_k and Z_ℓ. Each of the $\sigma_{i\ell}$ are assumed to be independent of the market prices p_k, total expenditures M and Z_ℓ, $j \neq \ell$.

---

as well.

By letting $\gamma_i = 0$ $i = 1, 2, \ldots, n$ with no loss in generality, the general form of the demand functions[2] derived from (6.1) satisfy

$$p_i X_i = \sum_{k=1}^{n} \beta_k M^{\sigma_{k0}} \left(\prod_{k=1}^{n} p_h^{\sigma_{kh}} \right) \left(\prod_{\ell-1}^{n} Z_\ell^{\tilde{\sigma}_{k\ell}} \right) \epsilon_k \frac{M}{p_i} \tag{6.6}$$

Defining expenditure shares as

$$M_i = \frac{p_i X_i}{M} \tag{6.7}$$

it follows immediately that

$$\frac{M_i}{M_k} = \frac{\beta_i}{\beta_k} M^{\sigma_{i0} - \sigma_{k0}} \prod_{j=1}^{n} p_j^{\sigma_{ij} - \sigma_{ik}} \prod_{\ell=1}^{m} Z_{e\ell\ell}^{\tilde{\sigma}_{i\ell} - \tilde{\sigma}_{k\ell}} \frac{\epsilon_i}{\epsilon_k} \tag{6.8}$$

The estimating system then is

$$\ln \left(\frac{M_i}{M_k} \right) = \ln \left(\frac{\beta_i}{\beta_k} \right) + \omega_{i,M}^{(k)} \ln M + \sum_{j=1}^{n} \omega_{i,p_j}^{(k)} \ln p_j$$

$$+ \sum_{\ell=1}^{m} \omega_{i,Z_\ell}^{(k)} \ln Z_\ell + \eta_i^{(k)} \tag{6.9}$$

where $\eta_i^{(k)} = \ln \epsilon_i - \ln \epsilon_k$ and $\eta_i^{(k)} = \rho \eta_{t-1,i} + u_{ti}$ where $-1 < \rho < 1$ and $u_{ti} \sim$ iid $N(0, \sigma_u^2 I)$ As can be seen from (6.9) we assume a first-order autoregressive process[3] and can estimate the $\omega_{i,p_j}^{(k)}$'s and $\omega_{j,M}^{(k)}$'s directly from the price and expenditure data.[4] The estimation procedure

---

[2]In general, this system does not possess the Slutsky (1915) properties. To impose these properties requires the restriction $\sigma_{ij} = \sigma$.

[3]See chapter II for the extension to the second order process.

[4]Maximum likelihood estimators of coefficients and variance matrix $Q^{(n)}$ are obtained by grid search over a family of autoregressive models of the random disturbances in (6.9), a distinct estimate being obtained for each specification in that family. The behavioral theory of random taste-changes underlying the specification of serial correlation hypotheses is given in a recent article (Basmann, 1985). Only two of the assumptions of that theory (Basmann, 1985, pp. 199-202) were used in obtaining the estimates shown in Tables 6.1-6.4 here. They imply that the random disturbances $\eta_i^{(k)}$, $k = 1, \ldots, n - 1$ follow a first-order autoregressive process. Consequently, the grid search for ML test statistics and estimators is over the interval $-1 < \rho < 1$.

is Gauss-Aitken generalized least squares. Gauss-Aitken estimates of the
intercepts and elasticity terms are unbiased, minimum variance and minimum generalized variance. Also the F-ratios for testing null hypotheses
are distributed exactly as Snedecor's F-statistics with determinate de-
grees of freedom, (Basmann, 1985). If any of the $\omega_{i,p_j}^{(k)}$'s, $\omega_{i,M}^{(k)}$'s or $\omega_{i,Z_\ell}^{(k)}$'s
are statistically different from zero then, as noted in chapter three, we
have detected a change in preferences, *e.g.* a secondary utility effect and
we interpret that as a "Veblen effect" (see Chapter 3).

6.3   Empirical Results

To test the model specified above, price and expenditure data are required.
The price series is a Laspeyres-type index. A weighted average of the
appropriate subgroups was used to aggregate to a five-commodity level.
The data include 5 general commodity groups outlined in chapter 3 and
data Appendix A.

   The Canadian data are for the 1949-1983 period. The Mexican data
are for 1947-1978. The U.S. data covers the 1947-1981 period. While a
minor discrepancy exists, we felt it better to analyze the full series for each
country than to lose degrees of freedom or to create spurious observations.

   Estimation of (6.9) for each country will allow us to examine the secondary utility effects and test for conspicuous consumption in each country. A priori we expect the effects to be largest in the more developed U.S.
and Canadian economies. These economies have higher average disposable incomes and are thus more likely to exhibit Veblen effects, *cf.* Veblen
(1899, p. 126).

   Testing for evidence of these secondary utility effects will be conducted
in a sequential manner. First we will examine each of the $\omega_{i,p_j}^{(k)}$ for statistical significance. This will provide evidence as to secondary utility effects
from the prices of particular goods. Specifically, when the price of the jth
good changes, we can test for a significant change in the MRS between i
and k. Next we inspect the $\omega_{i,M}^{(k)}$ for statistical significance. If found, this
provides additional information as to the causes of the secondary utility
effects. In this case, the cause would be a change in total expenditures.
Next, we determine the statistical impact of a change in foreign price, Z_ℓ,
on the preference structure. If $\omega_{i,Z_\ell}^{(k)}$ is statistically different from zero, then

we can conclude that changes in relative foreign prices cause changes in the MRS and create secondary utility effects.

Here we define the foreign to domestic price ratio as the foreign CPI divided by the domestic CPI. We are concerned only with the intercountry impact of the three countries under investigation in this study. Thus, we have only two foreign price ratio variables for each country. For Canada, Z_1 is the ratio of U.S. to Canadian prices and Z_2 is the ratio of Mexican to Canadian prices. For Mexico, Z_1 is the ratio of U.S. to Mexican prices and Z_2 is the ratio of Canadian to Mexican prices. For the U.S., Z_1 and Z_2 are the ratios of Mexican and Canadian to U.S. price ratios, respectively. In each case the numerator of the ratio is deflated by the appropriate exchange rate.

The next step in our testing procedure is to test for homogeneity with respect to prices:

$$\text{H}(1): \quad \sum_{j=1}^{5} \omega_{i,p_j}^{(k)} = 0 \tag{6.10}$$

This is a more restrictive test for secondary utility effects. A rejection of homogeneity indicates more strongly than an individually significant $\omega_{i,p_k}(\omega_{i,M}, \omega_{i,Z_\ell})$ that the preference structure has changed.

The final and strongest test for Veblen effects is a homogeneity test with respect to total expenditure and prices:

$$\text{H}(2): \quad \sum_{j=1}^{5} \omega_{i,p_j}^{(k)} + \omega_{i,M}^{(k)} = 0 \tag{6.11}$$

A rejection of H(2) collaborates the conclusion of changing preferences. The sequential testing procedure allows us to test for Veblen effects in an increasingly rigorous manner. One may not feel comfortable with the conclusion that secondary utility effects have occurred on the basis of a few statistically significant parameter estimates. H(1) is a more stringent tests of changes in the preference structure. A rejection on H(1) implies (6.1) is not invariant to changes in relative prices. The strongest test for secondary utility effects is H(2). In this case, a rejection of H(2) implies that (6.1) is not invariant to changes in real expenditures and prices.

The results of estimating (6.9) for Canada, Mexico and the U.S. are reported in Tables 6.1, 6.2, and 6.3. There is evidence of Veblen effects for nearly all goods in the U.S. and Canada. These secondary utility effects are twice as numerous for the U.S. (at the .05 significance level).

One might wonder however, if these Veblen effects have changed over time. For example, do we find a large number of Veblen effects in the early years of the U.S. data when real income was growing at a faster rate? Alternatively do the goods which exhibit Veblen effects vary depending on growth rates in real income? To test these hypotheses we divided each sample at the chronological midpoint. Chow tests were calculated to determine if the subsamples were from the same population.[5]

In several cases for Canada and the U.S. we find the null rejected at the .05 significance level, indicating a shift in the Veblen effects.

The discussion of the results will follow the sequential testing pattern outlined above. We first examine the parameter estimates for each country. We begin by discussing the results for the time period spanned by the data as well as the results of dividing the data. The parameter estimates are compared across countries. Finally the results of the homogeneity tests are compared for each country.

---

[5] The samples are

- Mexico: 1947 - 1962 and 1963 - 1978.
- Canada: 1949 - 1966 and 1967 - 1983.
- U.S.:   1947 - 1964 and 1965 - 1981.

Table 6.1
The MRS–Elasticities for Canada

For Numeraire= 1

	INT	$\omega_{i0}^{(1)}$	$\omega_{i1}^{(1)}$	$\omega_{i2}^{(1)}$	$\omega_{i3}^{(1)}$	$\omega_{i4}^{(1)}$	$\omega_{i5}^{(1)}$	$\omega_{iz_{(1)}}^{(1)}$	$\omega_{iz_{(2)}}^{(1)}$
CLOTHING	-5.880	0.430	-0.322	1.159	-0.536	-0.500	-0.003	0.067	-0.044
	(.0034)	(.0288)	(.1006)	(.0001)	(.2012)	(.0814)	(.9921)	(.6211)	(.4597)
HOUSING	3.490	-0.540	-0.571	-0.373	1.061	-0.284	1.045	0.154	0.030
	(.0136)	(.0004)	(.0003)	(.0381)	(.0013)	(.1671)	(.0001)	(.1212)	(.9763)
DURABLE	1.485	-0.557	1.151	-1.707	-2.046	2.186	0.527	-0.735	-0.152
	(.8430)	(.4657)	(.1452)	(.0880)	(.2293)	(.0616)	(.6634)	(.1851)	(.5276)
MEDICAL	-6.797	0.557	-0.204	-0.024	-0.339	0.282	-0.559	0.121	0.027
	(.0001)	(.0001)	(.1045)	(.8733)	(.2080)	(.1235)	(.0063)	(.1700)	(.4838)

For Numeraire= 2

	INT	$\omega_{i0}^{(2)}$	$\omega_{i1}^{(2)}$	$\omega_{i2}^{(2)}$	$\omega_{i3}^{(2)}$	$\omega_{i4}^{(2)}$	$\omega_{i5}^{(2)}$	$\omega_{iz_{(1)}}^{(2)}$	$\omega_{iz_{(2)}}^{(2)}$
HOUSING	9.370	-0.969	-0.250	-1.532	1.597	0.216	1.048	0.087	0.074
	(.0023)	(.0020)	(.3920)	(.0002)	(.0160)	(.6142)	(.0269)	(.6706)	(.4138)
DURABLE	7.366	-0.987	1.472	-2.866	-1.511	2.686	0.530	-0.802	-0.109
	(.4028)	(.2726)	(.1147)	(.0172)	(.4422)	(.0512)	(.7069)	(.2185)	(.6996)
MEDICAL	-0.916	0.127	0.117	-1.183	0.197	0.782	-0.556	0.053	0.070
	(.7069)	(.6004)	(.6421)	(.0007)	(.7143)	(.0390)	(.1586)	(.7589)	(.3606)

For Numeraire= 3

	INT	$\omega_{i0}^{(3)}$	$\omega_{i1}^{(3)}$	$\omega_{i2}^{(3)}$	$\omega_{i3}^{(3)}$	$\omega_{i4}^{(3)}$	$\omega_{i5}^{(3)}$	$\omega_{iz_{(1)}}^{(3)}$	$\omega_{iz_{(2)}}^{(3)}$
DURABLE	-2.004	-0.017	1.722	-1.334	-3.108	2.477	-0.518	-0.890	-0.183
	(.7892)	(.9842)	(.0314)	(.1729)	(.0695)	(.0343)	(.6634)	(.1085)	(.4422)
MEDICAL	-10.286	1.097	0.367	0.349	-1.400	0.566	-1.604	-0.033	-0.003
	(.0001)	(.0001)	(.0580)	(.1452)	(.0017)	(.0462)	(.0001)	(.8045)	(.5535)

For Numeraire= 4

	INT	$\omega_{i0}^{(4)}$	$\omega_{i1}^{(4)}$	$\omega_{i2}^{(4)}$	$\omega_{i3}^{(4)}$	$\omega_{i4}^{(4)}$	$\omega_{i5}^{(4)}$	$\omega_{iz_{(1)}}^{(4)}$	$\omega_{iz_{(2)}}^{(4)}$
MEDICAL	-8.282	1.114	-1.355	1.683	1.708	-1.904	-1.086	0.856	0.179
	(.2684)	(.1452)	(.0847)	(.0880)	(.3076)	(.0969)	(.3657)	(.1212)	(.4480)

Note: Actual derivation of the $\omega_{i.}^{(n)}$ and $\omega_{i0}^{(n)}$ and description of their estimation procedure is given in the text.

Table 6.2
The MRS–Elasticities for Mexico

For Numeraire= 1

	INT	$\omega_{i0}^{(1)}$	$\omega_{i1}^{(1)}$	$\omega_{i2}^{(1)}$	$\omega_{i3}^{(1)}$	$\omega_{i4}^{(1)}$	$\omega_{i5}^{(1)}$	$\omega_{iz_{(1)}}^{(1)}$	$\omega_{iz_{(2)}}^{(1)}$
CLOTHING	-1.685	0.091	-0.905	-0.418	0.646	-0.331	1.139	-0.424	0.389
	(.0156)	(.3505)	(.0281)	(.0358)	(.0103)	(.6211)	(.0471)	(.1642)	(.1328)
HOUSING	-0.087	0.106	-2.015	0.739	-0.628	1.526	0.123	0.166	-0.367
	(.9526)	(.6142)	(.0246)	(.0830)	(.2256)	(.2985)	(.9211)	(.7968)	(.5023)
DURABLE	-3.144	0.102	-1.012	-0.999	1.040	1.057	0.121	-0.290	0.404
	(.0281)	(.6073)	(.2220)	(.0168)	(.0407)	(.4480)	(.9054)	(.6421)	(.4422)
MEDICAL	-1.878	-0.066	-0.460	-0.616	0.633	0.427	0.323	0.106	-0.124
	(.0616)	(.6421)	(.4307)	(.0358)	(.0783)	(.6634)	(.6923)	(.8121)	(.7365)

For Numeraire= 2

	INT	$\omega_{i0}^{(2)}$	$\omega_{i1}^{(2)}$	$\omega_{i2}^{(2)}$	$\omega_{i3}^{(2)}$	$\omega_{i4}^{(2)}$	$\omega_{i5}^{(2)}$	$\omega_{iz_{(1)}}^{(2)}$	$\omega_{iz_{(2)}}^{(2)}$
HOUSING	1.598	0.016	-1.110	1.157	-1.274	1.857	-1.016	0.590	-0.756
	(.2810)	(.9447)	(.2149)	(.0108)	(.0215)	(.2185)	(.4138)	(.3813)	(.1882)
DURABLE	-1.459	0.012	0.107	-0.581	0.393	1.388	-1.018	0.134	0.015
	(.2330)	(.9447)	(.8819)	(.1045)	(.3657)	(.2602)	(.3168)	(.8045)	(.9763)
MEDICAL	-0.193	-0.157	0.445	-0.197	-0.013	0.758	-0.816	0.530	-0.513
	(.8352)	(.2602)	(.4307)	(.4657)	(.9684)	(.0001)	(.3030)	(.2185)	(.1614)

For Numeraire= 3

	INT	$\omega_{i0}^{(3)}$	$\omega_{i1}^{(3)}$	$\omega_{i2}^{(3)}$	$\omega_{i3}^{(3)}$	$\omega_{i4}^{(3)}$	$\omega_{i5}^{(3)}$	$\omega_{iz_{(1)}}^{(3)}$	$\omega_{iz_{(2)}}^{(3)}$
DURABLE	-3.057	-0.004	1.003	-1.738	1.668	-0.469	-0.001	-0.456	0.771
	(.1946)	(.9921)	(.4717)	(.0146)	(.0534)	(.8430)	(.9999)	(.6634)	(.3920)
MEDICAL	-1.791	-0.172	1.555	-1.355	1.261	-1.099	0.200	-0.600	0.243
	(.3974)	(.5801)	(.2256)	(.0343)	(.1045)	(.6073)	(.9132)	(.9526)	(.7665)

For Numeraire= 4

	INT	$\omega_{i0}^{(4)}$	$\omega_{i1}^{(4)}$	$\omega_{i2}^{(4)}$	$\omega_{i3}^{(4)}$	$\omega_{i4}^{(4)}$	$\omega_{i5}^{(4)}$	$\omega_{iz_{(1)}}^{(4)}$	$\omega_{iz_{(2)}}^{(4)}$
MEDICAL	1.266	-0.168	0.552	0.383	-0.407	-0.630	0.201	0.396	-0.528
	(.2522)	(.2985)	(.4028)	(.2330)	(.3030)	(.5734)	(.8275)	(.4250)	(.2149)

Note: Actual derivation of the $\omega_{is}^{(n)}$ and $\omega_{i0}^{(n)}$ and description of their estimation procedure is given in the text.

Table 6.3
The MRS–Elasticities for The United States

For Numeraire= 1

	INT	$\omega_{i0}^{(1)}$	$\omega_{i1}^{(1)}$	$\omega_{i2}^{(1)}$	$\omega_{i3}^{(1)}$	$\omega_{i4}^{(1)}$	$\omega_{i5}^{(1)}$	$\omega_{iz_{(1)}}^{(1)}$	$\omega_{iz_{(2)}}^{(1)}$
CLOTHING	-1.268	0.489	-0.458	0.236	-0.099	-0.139	-0.176	-0.027	-0.017
	(.0011)	(.0017)	(.0201)	(.2941)	(.7069)	(.5148)	(.3310)	(.7291)	(.6142)
HOUSING	-1.802	0.113	-0.281	-1.190	0.133	0.363	1.038	0.156	-0.109
	(.0050)	(.6351)	(.3761)	(.0037)	(.7665)	(.3168)	(.0019)	(.2444)	(.0580)
DURABLE	-5.940	2.220	-1.354	-0.842	0.817	0.168	-1.486	0.151	-0.055
	(.0001)	(.0001)	(.0004)	(.0452)	(.0969)	(.6634)	(.0001)	(.2941)	(.3606)
MEDICAL	-2.336	0.288	-0.523	-0.318	-0.513	0.124	1.147	-0.171	-0.070
	(.0001)	(.0915)	(.0230)	(.2293)	(.1065)	(.6211)	(.0001)	(.0724)	(.0768)

For Numeraire= 2

	INT	$\omega_{i0}^{(2)}$	$\omega_{i1}^{(2)}$	$\omega_{i2}^{(2)}$	$\omega_{i3}^{(2)}$	$\omega_{i4}^{(2)}$	$\omega_{i5}^{(2)}$	$\omega_{iz_{(1)}}^{(2)}$	$\omega_{iz_{(2)}}^{(2)}$
HOUSING	-0.534	-0.376	0.177	-1.426	0.232	0.502	1.214	0.183	-0.92
	(.3606)	(.1147)	(.5667)	(.0005)	(.5936)	(.1558)	(.0003)	(.1642)	(.0950)
DURABLE	-4.672	1.731	-0.896	-1.078	0.917	0.307	-1.310	0.178	-0.038
	(.0001)	(.0001)	(.0121)	(.0118)	(.0642)	(.4250)	(.0004)	(.2149)	(.5212)
MEDICAL	-1.068	-0.201	-0.065	-0.554	-0.414	0.263	1.323	-0.143	-0.054
	(.0139)	(.2293)	(.7665)	(.0407)	(.1882)	(.2897)	(.0001)	(.1258)	(.1671)

For Numeraire= 3

	INT	$\omega_{i0}^{(3)}$	$\omega_{i1}^{(3)}$	$\omega_{i2}^{(3)}$	$\omega_{i3}^{(3)}$	$\omega_{i4}^{(3)}$	$\omega_{i5}^{(3)}$	$\omega_{iz_{(1)}}^{(3)}$	$\omega_{iz_{(2)}}^{(3)}$
DURABLE	-4.138	2.107	-1.073	0.348	0.684	-0.194	-2.524	-0.005	0.54
	(.0001)	(.0001)	(.0068)	(.4307)	(.2012)	(.6421)	(.0001)	(.9763)	(.4083)
MEDICAL	-0.534	0.175	-0.242	0.872	-0.646	-0.239	0.109	-0.327	0.039
	(.1914)	(.2853)	(.2643)	(.0019)	(.0407)	(.3262)	(.6004)	(.0011)	(.3076)

For Numeraire= 4

	INT	$\omega_{i0}^{(4)}$	$\omega_{i1}^{(4)}$	$\omega_{i2}^{(4)}$	$\omega_{i3}^{(4)}$	$\omega_{i4}^{(4)}$	$\omega_{i5}^{(4)}$	$\omega_{iz_{(1)}}^{(4)}$	$\omega_{iz_{(2)}}^{(4)}$
MEDICAL	3.604	-1.931	0.831	0.523	-1.331	-0.044	2.633	-0.321	-0.016
	(.0001)	(.0001)	(.0153)	(.1820)	(.0070)	(.9054)	(.0001)	(.0246)	(.7816)

Note: Actual derivation of the $\omega_{i\bullet}^{(n)}$ and $\omega_{i0}^{(n)}$ and description of their estimation procedure is given in the text.

Table 6.4
Maximum Likelihood Tests of Restricted Models

	For Numeraire=Food						
	Clothing				Housing		
	Canada	Mexico	U.S.A.		Canada	Mexico	U.S.A.
$H(1)^*$	0.4891	2.3057	11.894	$H(1)$	17.7439	1.8747	0.0403
	(.4905)	(.1425)	(.0019)		(.0003)	(.1842)	(.8424)
$H(2)^{**}$	3.7360	7.5234	6.9593	$H(2)$	15.7371	0.7274	3.4750
	(.0642)	(.0116)	(.0139)		(.0005)	(.4025)	(.0736)
	Durable				Medical		
	Canada	Mexico	U.S.A.		Canada	Mexico	U.S.A.
$H(1)$	0.0088	1.3493	65.5665	$H(1)$	20.8973	5.8444	0.1516
	(.9259)	(.2573)	(.0001)		(.0001)	(.0240)	(.7002)
$H(2)$	0.8735	3.4313	22.3145	$H(2)$	14.5089	4.1029	9.7901
	(.3586)	(.0768)	(.0001)		(.0008)	(.0546)	(.0043)
	For Numeraire=Clothing						
	Housing						
	Canada	Mexico	U.S.A.				
$H(1)$	6.0581	4.0392	5.326				
	(.0208)	(.0563)	(.0292)				
$H(2)$	0.3768	4.2347	12.415				
	(.5447)	(.0511)	(.0016)				
	Durable				Medical		
	Canada	Mexico	U.S.A.		Canada	Mexico	U.S.A.
$H(1)$	0.0516	0.2341	38.480	$H(1)$	2.9204	2.0830	6.624
	(.8222)	(.6331)	(.0001)		(.0994)	(.1624)	(.0161)
$H(2)$	1.4472	0.3547	10.699	$H(2)$	11.2402	0.0294	29.3089
	(.2398)	(.5573)	(.0030)		(.0025)	(.8653)	(.0001)
	For Numeraire=Housing						
	Durable				Medical		
	Canada	Mexico	U.S.A.		Canada	Mexico	U.S.A.
$H(1)$	0.4403	2.3218	57.2089	$H(1)$	37.0570	4.1540	0.4835
	(.5128)	(.1412)	(.0001)		(.0001)	(.0532)	(.4930)
H(2)	2.7535	2.5991	34.8508	$H(2)$	29.2571	2.2766	0.2025
	(.1091)	(.1206)	(.0001)		(.0001)	(.1450)	(.6564)
	For Numeraire=Durable						
	Medical						
	Canada	Mexico	U.S.A.				
$H(1)$	0.6847	0.4914	67.0735				
	(.4155)	(.4903)	(.0001)				
$H(2)$	0.1142	0.2596	49.6746				
	(.7381)	(.6152)	(.0001)				

NOTE:

* $H(1)$ is the null hypothesis that prices are homogenous of degree zero, i.e., $H(1): \sum_{j=1}^{5} \omega_{ij}^{(k)} = 0$, $i = 1, 2, \ldots, 5, k = 1, 2, \ldots, 5$.

** $H(2)$ is the null hypothesis that prices and income are homogenous of degree zero, i.e., $H(2):$ $\sum_{j=1}^{5} \omega_{ij}^{(k)} + \omega_{iM}^{(k)} = 0, i = 1, 2, \ldots, 5, k = 1, 2, \ldots, 5$.

Both tests are distributed as the F-distribution. The number in parenthesis is the Prob $F >$ $F_{q,n-K}/H(i) = 0; i = 1, 2$

Beginning with the Canadian results we note that while there are 13 parameter estimates which indicate Veblen effects, none of these are for the durables group. However, evidence of these effects are equally predominant for each of the other goods. Although the price of clothing and the price of medical goods each accounted for over 20% of the secondary utility effects, total expenditure changes most frequently cause shifts in the MRS. We find no indication that foreign prices impact Canadian demand for the commodities considered here.

We split the data at the chronological midpoint to examine if Veblen effects were more or less visible during different time periods. A summary of the results are discussed below. The number of significant parameters for the later years is about half of that for the earlier years. A switch in goods exhibiting Veblen effects seems to have occurred. Whereas food, clothing, housing and medical groups exhibit these effects 1949-1966, housing dominates these effects in the post 1966 sample. As food and medical services are not highly visible consumption goods for many, then commodities like housing can be expected to show stronger Veblen effects, *cf.* Veblen (1899).

As one might suspect, due to lack of discretionary income, there are very few significant $\omega_{i,p_j}^{(k)}$'s in the Mexico results. There is little evidence of Veblen effects in the Mexican Economy. Each of the four cases that were observed was in conjunction with food expenditures. The price of food and the price of housing cause the most significant shifts in the MRS. Given relatively low wealth levels, one would not expect to observe conspicuous consumption except by a very few. Concurrently, if any Veblen effects occur in Mexico in general, they would probably be in commodities that people require anyway, like clothing and food. The results of the chow test indicate that splitting the sample is inappropriate, i.e., the null can not be rejected. A shift in Veblen effects has not occurred for the Mexican economy.

Turning to the U.S. results (see Table 6.3) we find a preponderance of statistically significant parameter estimates for each commodity, including the durables group.

We also find indication of Veblen effects in response to changes in Mexican and Canadian prices. It is interesting to note that food prices, clothing prices and medical prices are most often the causes of shifts in the MRS. Changes in expenditures also caused changes in the MRS, particularly for durable goods.

Again, the data is split to determine if any of these results are time dependent. Similarly to the Canadian results, there is a dramatic decline in the number of statistically significant coefficients between 1949-1966 and 1967-1981. Veblen effects are indicated for all goods during the period 1949-1966. In the later periods the strongest effects seem to be for medical goods. Also, in the earlier period all commodity price changes (except P_4) indicate Veblen effects. In the more recent period medical prices and total expenditures most frequently cause the shifts. Finally, we note that in certain cases it is clear there hasn't been a shift in Veblen effects but consistent evidence of conspicuous consumption, e.g. $\omega_{3,p_3}^{(5)}$, $\omega_{3,p_5}^{(5)}$, $\omega_{2,p_5}^{(5)}$ and $\omega_{2,M}^{(1)}$.

We conclude that for poorer economies, e.g. Mexico, the conspicuous consumption effect, if any, will occur in a commodity like food which is relatively less expensive and not particularly lumpy in consumption.[6] In the more wealthy economies we find conspicuous consumption occurs for more expensive goods, however the most lumpy of expenditure categories, durables, still do not exhibit large secondary utility effects.

We find a similar pattern in terms of total expenditures. We find no evidence of secondary utility effects for total expenditures in Mexico. There is some evidence of these effects in Canada and even more so for the U.S. Given the relative average wealth levels among the three economies, our results are not surprising.

The dramatic shift in Veblen effects for the split sample is somewhat surprising. The results indicate that either real disposable income didn't increase as rapidly in the later years or there was a redistribution of wealth which reduced the number of Veblen effects. Unfortunately our sample size prevents any sensitivity analysis of the break year.

We continue our sequential testing by examining the results of the homogeneity tests. These tests reported in Table 6.4 collaborate our results. H(1) is the null hypothesis that $\sum \omega_{i,p_j}^{(k)}$ for each commodity in each country is equal to zero. H(2) is the null hypothesis of homogeneity with respect to income and prices, i.e. $\sum \omega_{ij}^{(k)} + \omega_{i0}^{(k)} = 0$. The results of homogeneity tests, H(1) (and H(2)), are by definition symmetric. For example,

---

[6]By "lumpy consumption", we mean the notion of goods that are not purchased continuously, like food, but rather are purchased in "lumps" like automobiles.

H(1) for numeraire = food, commodity = clothing is identical to H(1) for numeraire = clothing, commodity = food. In only three cases (at the 5 percent significance level) does Mexico reject the hypothesis of homogeneity, either with respect to prices or with respect to prices and income.[7] On the other hand, Canada and U.S. repeatedly reject both homogeneity hypotheses. Based on the number of times the hypothesis is rejected, the U.S. appears to have more Veblen effects when all prices or real income are changing. Since the homogeneity tests can be interpreted as being a stronger test, one may tentatively conclude that U.S. citizens exhibit more Veblen effects. Given that U.S. citizens have a higher level of disposable income, this is a plausible result.

6.4 Chapter Summary

This chapter examines price dependent preferences for the three North American countries. It was hypothesized that the more developed countries, Canada and the U.S., would exhibit stronger Veblen effects. Our results support this hypothesis. Furthermore, we conclude that the goods exhibiting Veblen effects differ, indicating differences in consumer tastes and preference structures between the two countries. In addition, we find evidence of time varying Veblen effects for Canada and the U.S.

We also examined the effect of foreign prices on preferences. We found strong Veblen effects only for the U.S. Although our results do not indicate the precise direction and magnitude of the changes in demand or consumer welfare, one might speculate that at least some foreign goods have conspicuous consumption qualities or Scitovsky quality-signalling characteristics for U.S. consumers. To the extent that free trade policies result in lower prices, utility from these goods may be changed. Of course, real income will be increased and this will have a positive effect on welfare. The net welfare effect is ambiguous with respect to the prices changes.

---

[7]In Table 6.4, there are six cases where the test is significant. Because of the symmetry explained above, three are redundant.

Chapter 7

Testing for Habit Persistence

7.1 Introduction

Marshall long ago noted the phenomenon of past consumption being highly correlated with current consumption. If "habit" was indeed a major determinant of current consumption behavior, then the neo-classical theory of utility maximization should take it into account. A rigorous incorporation of habit formation into consumer theory began with the work of Gorman (1967). Pollak (1976, 1977) laid out the theoretical conditions that needed to be satisfied in order for "habit persistence" to be consistent with the utility maximizing model of consumer behavior.

Empirical work in this area was competently done initially by Houthakker and Taylor (1970) with subsequent studies by Manser (1976), Phlips (1972), Pollak and Wales (1969) and Blanciforti and Green (1984). These papers have focused on examining the impact of measured past consumption on current consumption. One approach (Pollak 1976) for examining past consumption has been to incorporate "habit" into a subsistence parameter.

In this chapter we present a model which allows us to examine the impact of past consumption behavior on the current structure of preferences. Specifically, our model allows past ratios of expenditures on various commodity groups and lagged quantities of commodities to impact the elasticity of the marginal rate at which consumers substitute one commodity group for another. We present this model in section two. In section three we present the empirical results of the chapter. The innovation here is the use of a direct utility function that allows us to trace how past consumption or "habit persistence" affects the current preference structure. We summarize the chapter in section four.

7.2   The Model

In the standard neoclassical approach, only quantities of commodities determine the preference function. In order to test for habit persistence by consumers we must first develop a model in which lagged commodities can have some impact on current preferences.

In this chapter we adopt a methodology first proposed by Basmann (1954). In his chapter, Basmann provided a theoretical foundation for our model. Subsequently, Basmann, Molina and Slottje (1983) presented a framework for empirically testing for preferences which depended on prices and expenditures as well as quantities. This methodology is extended here to investigate the existence of habit persistence by consumers. We proceed by summarizing the Basmann methodology and developing our extension.

Let $U(X; \alpha)$ again be a direct utility function with continuous second partial derivatives with respect to X, where a designates the vector of all its parameters. Let $R_i^{(n)}(X; \alpha)$ $i, \ldots, n-1$ designate the marginal rate of substitution of X_n for X_i at the point X. Let α_k, $k = 1, \ldots, m$ be an observable magnitude different from X and its components. Assume that the direct utility function and all its first and second partial derivatives, U_i and U_{ij}, are differentiable at least once at all points (X) of the budget domain with respect to each of the preference changing variables $\alpha_1, \ldots, \alpha_m$. Then each of the marginal rates of substitution $R_i^{(n)}$, $i = 1, \ldots, n-1$ is differentiable at every point (X) of the domain with respect to each preference-changing variable α_k, $k = 1, 2, \ldots, m$. Following Ichimura (1951) and Tintner (1960), we define α_k to be a preference-changing variable for $U(X; \alpha)$ at X, and

$$\frac{\partial R_i^{(n)}}{\partial \alpha_k} \neq 0 \qquad (7.1)$$
$$i = 1, 2, \ldots, n-1$$
$$k = 1, 2, \ldots, m$$

for at least one i at X. We can express the effect of a change of one economic magnitude on another in terms of mathematical elasticities. Let the elasticity of the marginal rate of substitution (M.R.S.) of X_n for X_i with respect to a change in α be defined as

$$\omega_{i,\alpha_k}^{(n)} = \frac{\alpha_k}{R_i^{(n)}} \frac{\partial R_i^{(n)}}{\partial \alpha_k} \tag{7.2}$$
$$i = 1, 2, \ldots, n-1$$
$$k = 1, 2, \ldots, m$$

Given Hicks (1946) exposition of the relation between the marginal rate of substitution and marginal utilities:

$$R_i^{(n)} = \frac{U_i}{U_n} \tag{7.3}$$

where U_i and U_n are marginal utilities of X_i and X_n respectively. Define σ_{h,α_k} as the elasticity of the marginal utilities with respect to a preference-changing variable α_k:

$$\sigma_{\alpha_k} = \frac{\alpha_k}{U_h} \frac{\partial U_h}{\partial \alpha_k}$$
$$i = 1, 2, \ldots, n-1$$
$$k = 1, 2, \ldots, m$$

The elasticities of the M.R.S. (7.3), with respect to a change in α_j are in general:

$$\omega_{i,\alpha_j}^{(k)} = \frac{\alpha_j}{R_i^{(k)}} \frac{\partial R_i^{(k)}}{\partial \alpha_j} \tag{7.4}$$
$$= \frac{\alpha_j}{U_i} \frac{\partial U_i}{\partial \alpha_j} - \frac{\alpha_j}{U_k} \frac{\partial U_k}{\partial \alpha_j}$$
$$= \sigma_{ij} - \sigma_{kj}$$

To test for the existence of "habit persistence effects" we need to define a direct utility function in which past consumption can have an explicit impact on the parameters of the utility function. We specify a functional form for $U(X; \alpha)$ for which the preference changing variables are a function of past period expenditures and quantities. One such form is the Generalized Fechner-Thurstone (GFT) direct utility function. In this chapter we use a special form of the GFT, specifically we utilize a constant elasticity of marginal rate of substitution (CEMRS) form. Let

$$U(X;\theta) \;=\; \prod_{i=1}^{n} X_i^{\theta_i} \tag{7.5}$$

$$\sum_{i=1}^{n} \theta_i \;=\; \theta$$

be defined to be a GFT direct utility function. The parameter θ_i can be a function of any set of variables hypothesized to impact $U(X;\theta)$. Since we are interested in past consumption effects we can define θ to be a function of the quantities consumed of the X_i in one lagged period, $\hat{X}_i$. Following earlier work by Basmann et al. (1983) we will also include the vector of prices, p_i, and total expenditures, M,

$$\theta_i = \beta_i M^{\sigma_{ij}} \left(\prod_{j=1}^{n} p_j^{\sigma_{ij}} \right) \left(\prod_{j=1}^{n} \hat{X}_j^{\lambda_{ij}} \right) e^{u_i} \tag{7.6}$$

where the error term u_i is assumed to be *iid* $\mathrm{N}(0,\sigma^2 \mathrm{I})$. Here $\hat{X}_j$ represents the lagged one period quantity of the jth good.

Maximization of U subject to a budget constraint yields

$$X_i = \frac{\beta_i M^{\sigma_{i0}} \prod_{j=1}^{n} p_j^{\sigma_{ij}} \prod_{q=1}^{n} \hat{X}_q^{\lambda_{iq}} e^{u_i}}{K(p,M,\hat{X},)p_i} M \tag{7.7}$$

where

$$K(\bullet) = \sum_{k=1}^{n} \beta_k M^{\sigma_{i0}} \prod_{j=1}^{n} p_j^{\sigma_{jk}} \prod_{q=1}^{n} \hat{X}_q^{\lambda_{iq}} e^{u_k}$$

To estimate (7.7) we take the ratio of the expenditure shares, M_i, in loglinear form:

$$\ln \frac{M_i}{M_k} = \ln \frac{\beta_i}{\beta_k} + \omega_{i0}^{(k)} \ln M + \sum_{j=1}^{n} \omega_{ij}^{(k)} \ln p_j + \sum_{j=1}^{n} \gamma_{ij}^{(k)} \ln \hat{X}_j + \eta_i^{(k)} \tag{7.8}$$

where

$$\begin{aligned}
\omega_{i0}^{(k)} &= \sigma_{i0} - \sigma_{k0} \\
\omega_{ij}^{(k)} &= \sigma_{ij} - \sigma_{kj} \\
\gamma_{ij}^{(k)} &= \lambda_{ij} - \lambda_{kj} \\
\eta_i^{(k)} &= \ln u_i - \ln u_k
\end{aligned} \tag{7.9}$$

While specifying habit formation in terms of $\hat{X}_i$ has been the most popular form in the literature, sometimes lagged expenditures have been used. We can define θ alternatively in such a way as to derive an estimating equation which can be tested as an AR(1). In this case θ_i is defined as

$$\theta_i = \beta_i M^{\sigma_{i0}} \prod_{j=1}^{n} p_j^{\sigma_{ij}} \prod_{j=1}^{n} \hat{\theta}_j^{\varsigma_{ij}} e^{u_i} \qquad (7.10)$$

The estimating form for this specification is

$$\ln \frac{M_i}{M_k} = \ln \frac{\beta_i}{\beta_k} + \omega_{i0}^{(k)} \ln M + \sum_{j=1}^{n} \omega_{ij}^{(k)} \ln p_j + \sum_{j=1}^{n} \delta_{ij}^{(k)} \ln \frac{\hat{M}_i}{\hat{M}_k} + \eta_i^{(k)} \quad (7.11)$$

where $\delta_{ij}^{(k)} = \varsigma_{ij} - \varsigma_{kj}$. This specification allows us to examine habit persistence modelled as the lagged period ratio of expenditures on the various commodity groups. We assume a second-order autoregressive process for each specification for both (7.8) and (7.11), i.e., $\eta_{ti}^{(k)} = \rho_i \eta_{t-1,i} + \rho_2 \eta_{t-2,i} + \epsilon_t$. The parameters can be estimated directly from the price and expenditure data. The estimation procedure is Gauss-Aitken generalized least squares. Gauss-Aitken estimates of the intercepts and elasticity terms are unbiased, minimum variance and minimum generalized variance. Also the F-ratios for testing null hypotheses are distributed exactly as Snedecor's F-statistics with determinate degrees of freedom, (Basmann, 1985). If any of the γ_{ij}'s or δ_{ij}'s are statistically different from zero then we have detected a change in the elasticity of the MRS due to lagged quantities or ratios of expenditures lagged. We interpret these as habit persistence effects.

7.3   Empirical Results

To test the model specified above, price and expenditure data are required. The price series is a Laspeyres-type index. A weighted average of the appropriate subgroups was used to aggregate to a five-commodity level. The data include 5 general commodity groups outlined in Appendix A and mentioned in section 3.1. Testing for evidence of these habit persistence effects will be conducted in the following manner. First we will examine each of the γ_{ij}'s for statistical significance. This will provide evidence as to secondary utility effects from lagged quantities. Specifically, we can test for a significant change in the MRS between i and k when past quantities change. Next we inspect the δ_{ij} for statistical significance. If found, this provides additional information as to the causes of the habit persistence effects. In this case, the cause would be a change in previous expenditure ratios on two particular commodity groups.

The model laid out in Section II above allows us to be able to estimate habit persistence effects directly. Actual estimation of the model specified in equations (7.5-7.8) was done as noted above, with a maximum likelihood procedure that took into account first and second order autocorrelation. Recalling our definition of a habit persistence effect, we can see that irregardless of whether we specified the lagged quantities of various commodities or lagged ratios of expenditures on commodities we get statistically significant effects. This can be seen from perusal of Tables 7.1 and 7.2. We report the results for the numeraire equal to medical care because we only want to demonstrate the technique and by the symmetry of (7.8) one can recover other estimates if so desired.

In Table 7.1 we present the results for the case where the habit persistence is confined to lagged quantities of the various commodity groups in question. In this case we find statistically significant coefficient estimates in 40% of the cases. Consumption of four of the five commodities in the previous period had a statistically significant impact on the rate at which medical care is substituted for durables. Since durable goods are frequently non-necessities, it isn't surprising to see people adjusting the rate at which durables substitute for other goods (here medical care) given their preponderance of habitual consumption. Also of interest is the fact that clothing consumption in the previous period affected the marginal rates of substitution of medical care for each of the other goods. Apparently clothing is an activity associated with strong habitual behavior. We also observe strong lagged effects for housing and durables. Medical care and food consumption appear to be the least habitual.

In Table 7.2 we present the results for the case where medical care is the numeraire good. That is, we examine the impact of changes in the lagged ratios of expenditures of various commodities to medical care on the rate at which the various commodities are substituted for medical care. Intuitively, we are asking what happens to the rate at which aggregate consumers will exchange (say) medical care for clothing when the rate at which they purchase the two goods changes. From Table 7.2 we can see that the rate at which medical care is substituted for food increases (a positive coefficient), and strongly so (coefficient estimate is greater than one) and is a statistically significant effect at the .0001 level when the ratio of food to medical care expenditures increases. The rate at which medical care is substituted for housing seems to be impacted the most by lagged effects of changes in the ratios of expenditures of clothing, housing and durables to medical care. One explanation for this is that when people incorporate habits into their current consumption behavior, then they have to adjust their behavior (reflected here in the rate at which one good is substituted for another in the current period) to take account of habitual expenditures.

Homogeneity tests were completed for each specification. Our results indicate that we can reject the hypothesis at any reasonable significance level. The likelihood ratio test statistic had a value of 24.7051 with a probability level of $.5766 \times 10^{-4}$ for the first specification. The specification with lagged ratios of expenditures rejected the homogeneity test at the $.4131 \times 10^{-5}$ level. The test statistic was 30.3614.

A comparison of the likelihood values for each model indicates that the lagged consumption model performs better in a statistical sense.

7.4   Chapter Summary

This chapter has presented a flexible form of direct utility function that allows habit persistence to be incorporated into the behavioral specification. We tested the model with aggregate U.S. data and found our hypothesis to be in excellent agreement with the data. We found evidence of habit persistence affecting preferences across all goods examined in this chapter.

Table 7.1
Coefficient Estimates of Habit Persistence Effects of Past Period Quantities on the Elasticity of the Marginal Rate of Substitution for Various Commodity Groups

Elasticity of Marginal Rate of Substitution of	W.R.T. INT	Price Food	Price Clothing	Price Housing	Price Durables	Price Medical Care	Total Expenditures
Medical Care for Food	.7607 (.0007)	-.5263 (.1147)	-.6979 (.0007)	.2781 (.0237)	-.3646 (.1352)	.7000 (.0127)	-.2579 (.3580)
Medical Care for Clothing	.1077 (.5962)	-.0247 (.9419)	-.7675 (.0004)	.2056 (.0997)	-.8118 (.0033)	.9391 (.0021)	-.3292 (.2639)
Medical Care for Housing	.0846 (.5616)	-.4790 (.0585)	.2652 (.0589)	.3391 (.0007)	-.7093 (.0006)	.3037 (.1305)	-.4177 (.0547)
Medical Care for Durables	.1456 (.5689)	-1.2188 (.0085)	-.9785 (.0004)	.8606 (.0001)	-.3896 (.2214)	1.7533 (.0001)	-.7714 (.0444)

Elasticity of Marginal Rate of Substitution of	Previous Period of Quantity of Food	Previous Period of Quantity of Clothing	Previous Period of Quantity of Housing	Previous Period of Quantity of Durables	Previous Period of Quantity Md. Care
Medical Care for Food	.0713 (.5939)	-.7604 (.0082)	-.2075 (.1688)	-.4814 (.0164)	.0235 (.9637)
Medical Care for Clothing	.5537 (.0006)	-.5256 (.0678)	-.3142 (.0512)	-.2098 (.2905)	-.1431 (.7913)
Medical Care for Housing	-.1428 (.1623)	.4616 (.0280)	.0330 (.7652)	-.3861 (.0109)	.6469 (.1054)
Medical Care for Durables	-.2891 (.1101)	-.9291 (.0132)	.4759 (.0213)	-.9660 (.0007)	-2.2539 (.0029)

Note: $H : \ln \frac{\theta_i}{\theta_n} = \ln \frac{\beta_i}{\beta_n} + \omega_{i0}^{(n)} \ln M + \sum_{j=1}^{n} \omega_{ij}^{(n)} \ln P + \sum_{q=1}^{n} \omega_{i,X_q}^{(n)} \ln X_q + \nu_i^{(n)}$

Table 7.2
Coefficient Estimates of Habit Persistence Effects of Past
Period Ratios of Expenditures on the Elasticity of the
Marginal Rate of Substitution for Various Commodity Groups

Elasticity of Marginal Rate of Substitution of	W.R.T. INT	Price Food	Price Clothing	Price Housing	Price Durables	Price Medical Care	Total Expenditures
Medical Care for Food	.3950 (.0046)	.0809 (.7222)	-.3290 (.0333)	.2492 (.0480)	-.4902 (.0013)	-.0986 (.5112)	.3532 (.0252)
Medical Care for Clothing	-.0514 (.6695)	.2475 (.2564)	-.3006 (.0392)	.1308 (.2583)	-.6809 (.0001)	.2975 (.0442)	-.2325 (.1092)
Medical Care for Housing	.1351 (.1870)	.1202 (.5049)	.1544 (.1914)	-.1006 (.2964)	-.3050 (.0083)	-.0673 (.5696)	-.3172 (.0121)
Medical Care for Durables	-.1306 (.5439)	.3814 (.3245)	-.7670 (.0047)	.2816 (.1747)	-.6214 (.0122)	.5606 (.0342)	.0333 (.8945)

Elasticity of Marginal Rate of Substitution of	Ratio Expenditures in Previous Period of Food / Med. Care	Ratio Expenditures in Previous Period of Clothing / Med. Care	Ratio Expenditures in Previous Period of Housing / Med. Care	Ratio Expenditures in Previous Period of Durables / Med. Care
Medical Care for Food	.1508 (.2189)	-.1234 (.2333)	.1376 (.1025)	1.2581 (.0001)
Medical Care for Clothing	.7829 (.0001)	.0328 (.7339)	-.0275 (.7225)	.5971 (.0203)
Medical Care for Housing	.1205 (.2133)	.6566 (.0001)	.2623 (.0004)	.4882 (.0349)
Medical Care for Durables	-.0468 (.8179)	-.0345 (.8410)	.9161 (.0001)	-.6572 (.1372)

Note: $H : \ln \frac{\theta_i}{\theta_n} = \ln \frac{\beta_i}{\beta_n} + \omega_{i0}^{(n)} \ln M + \sum_{j=1}^{n} \omega_{ij}^{(n)} \ln P + \sum_{q=1}^{n} \omega_{i,X_q}^{(n)} \ln X_q + \nu_i^{(n)}$

Chapter 8

Concluding Remarks

This book has demonstrated that a direct utility function that is specified so as to include preferences that "are variable" has many diverse applications. While we have presented several of these applications here, we have by no means exhausted the possibilities. We now suggest some additional lines of research that we believe have sufficient merit to warrant future considerations.

One obvious area where the GFT form of utility function has interesting implications is with respect to social welfare functions. The same arguments discussed in the context of aggregate consumers tastes can be applied to a social welfare mapping where (say) the provision of public goods can be analyzed when (say) the relative price of one of the public goods changes.

Basmann *et al.* (1984 a-b) have briefly discussed a theoretical linkup between the GFT form of direct utility function and analysis of economic inequality. It is well known that a vital piece is missing, in the inequality literature on how a given distribution of economic well being is related to the underlying preference structure of the individuals that comprise the distribution. It will be shown in future research that by considering a multidimensional distribution of economic wellbeing, the conditional expectations of several of the variates (such as income and expenditures) depend on parameters of the GFT direct utility function. This research will be explored by the authors over the next few years.

A natural analog to the GFT direct utility function as we have explicated it above, is the GFT production function. The same theoretical

construct that allowed as to discuss Veblen effects and quality signalling
on the consumer side can be interpreted as technological-change parameters on the production side. The authors are currently beginning research
on this topic as well. Many other applications exist and we leave it to
the creative reader to develop new uses as he or she progresses with the
theory.

Finally, we conclude by pointing out that consumer theory is at a
crossroads. As Deaton and Muellbauer (1980b) note,

> Consumer behavior is frequently presented in terms of pref-
> erence, on the one hand, and possibilities on the other. The
> emphasis in the discussion is commonly placed on preferences
> .... The specification of which choices are actually available is
> given a secondary place and, frequently, only very simple possi-
> bilities are considered .... We begin, however, with the limits
> to choice rather than with the choices themselves. (1980b, p.3)

What we have attempted to do in this book is recognize the importance
of constraints (choices) and how that changes in these constraints affect
preferences.

While the assumption of fixed preferences may be convenient, economic
science must evolve to capture as broad a theory of consumer behavior as
possible in order to not become an archaic discipline. The GFT direct
utility function is one vehicle that allows us to drive in the right direction.

Bibliography

Afriat, S. N., "On the Constructability of Consistent Price Indices Between Several Periods Simultaneously," in *Essays in the Theory and Measurement of Consumer Behavior*, ed. Angus Deaton. Cambridge: Cambridge University Press, 1981.

Aitken, A. C., "On Least Squares and Linear Combinations of Observations," Proc. Royal Society of Edinburgh, Vol. 55, 1935: 42-48.

Arrow, Kenneth J., "Additive Logarithmic Demand Functions and the Slutsky Relations," *Review of Economic Studies*, Vol. 28, 1961: 176-181.

Arrow, Kenneth J., *Social Choice and Individual Values*, 2nd ed., New Haven, CT: Yale University Press, 1963.

Barnett, W. A., "Economic Monetary Aggregates: An Application of Index Numbers and Aggregation Theory," *Journal of Econometrics* Vol 14, 1980: 11-48.

Barnett, W. A., *Consumer Demand and Labor Supply,* Amsterdam: North Holland, 1981.

Barnett, W. A., "New Indices of Money Supply and the Flexible Laurent Demand System," *Journal of Business and Economic Statistics* Vol. 1, 1983: 7-23.

Barnett, W. A., "The Miniflex-Laurent Flexible Functional Form," *Journal of Econometrics*, Vol. 30, 1985: 1421-1438.

Barnett, W. A. and Lee, Yul W., "The Global Properties of the Miniflex Laurent, Generalized Leontief, and Translog Flexible Functional Forms," *Econometrica*, Vol. 53, 1985: 411-413.

Barten, A. P., "Theorie en empirie van een volledig stelsel van vraegvergelijkingen," PhD Thesis, Rotterdam: University of Rotterdam, 1966.

Barten, A. P., "Systems of Consumer Demand Functions Approach: A Review," *Econometrica*, Vol. 45, 1977: 23-51.

Barten, A. P., and Geyskens, "The Negativity Condition in Consumer Demand," *European Economic Review*, Vol. 6, 1975: 227-260.

Basmann, R. L., "Applications of Several Econometric Techniques to a Theory of Demand with variable Tastes," Ph.D. Dissertation, Iowa State College, 1955.

Basmann, R. L., "A Note on an Invariant Property of Shifts in Demand," *Metroeconomica*, Vol. 6, 1954: 69-71.

Basmann, R. L., "A Note in Mr. Ichimura's Definition of Related Goods," *Review of Economic Studies*, Vol. 22, 1954-55: 67-69.

Basmann, R. L., "A Theory of Demand with Variable consumer Preferences," *Econometrica*, Vol. 24, 1956: 47-59.

Basmann, R. L., "Hypothesis Formulation in Quantitative Economics: A Contribution to Demand Analysis," *Papers in Quantitative Economics*, Lawrence, KS: University Press of Kansas, 1968.

Basmann, R. L., "On the Serial Correlation of Stochastic Taste Changers in Direct Utility Functions," *Econometric Theory*, Vol. 1, 1985: 192-210.

Basmann, R. L., Diamond, C. A., Frentrup, J. C., and White, S. N., "Variable Consumer Preferences, Economic Inequality, and the Cost of Living, Part Two," in *Advances in Econometrics*, Vol. IV, ed. R. L. Basmann, and G. F. Rhodes, Jr., New York: JAI Press, 1985a: 1-85.

Basmann, R. L., Diamond, C. A., Frentrup, J. C., and White, S. N., "On Deviations Between Neoclassical and GFT-Based TCLI's Derived from the Same Demand System," *Journal of Econometrics*, Vol. 30, 1985b: 45-66.

Basmann, R.L., Diamond, C.A., and D.J. Slottje, "The Cost-of- Living Concept and COLAs", unpublished mimeo, Clemson University, 1988a.

Basmann, R.L., Diamond, C.A., and D.J. Slottje, "Relative Price Changes, Cost of Living Adjustments and their Redistributional Effects," unpublished mimeo, Clemson University, 1988b.

Basmann, R. L., Johnson, J. D. and Slottje D. J., "Alternative Utility Function Specification, Estimation and Likelihood Support," Working Paper #, Department of Economics, Southern Methodist University, Dallas, TX 75275, 1988.

Basmann, R. L., Molina, D. J., and Slottje, D. J., "Budget Constraint Prices as Preference Changing Parameters of Generalized Fechner-Thurstone Direct Utility Functions." *American Economic Review*, Vol. 73, 1983: pp. 411-413.

Basmann, R. L., Molina, D. J. and Slottje, D. J., "A Note on Aggregation of Fechner-Thurstone Direct Utility Functions," *Economic Letters*, Vol. 14, 1984a: 117-122.

Basmann, R. L., Molina, D. J., and Slottje, D. J., "Variable Consumer Preferences, Economic Inequality, and Cost of Living, Part One," Advances in Econometrics, Vol. III, ed. R. L. Basmann, and G. F. Rhodes, Jr., New York: JAI Press, 1984b: 1-69.

Basmann, R. L., Molina, D. J., and Slottje, D. J., "The GFT Direct Utility Function: An Exposition," *Journal of Institutional and Theoretical Economics*, Vol. 143, # 4, 1987: 568-594.

Basmann, R. L., Molina, D. J., and Slottje, D. J., "A Note on Measuring Veblen's Theory of Conspicuous Consumption," *Review of Economics and Statistics*, (forthcoming).

Basmann, R. L. and Slottje, D. J., "Significance of the Nonuniqueness of Neoclassical Direct Utility Functions Especially When They are Empirically Confirmed," Working Paper #8521, Department of Economics, Southern Methodist University, Dallas, TX 75275, 1985.

Basmann, R. L. and Slottje, D. J., "The Sensitivity of the Cost of Living Indexes to Price and Income Induced Changes of Aggregate Consumer Tastes," *Journal of Business and Economic Statistics*, Vol. 5, 1987: 483-498.

Basmann, R. L. and White, "Stigler's Challenge and a Terse Derivation of the Law of Demand," Public Policy Resources Laboratory, College of Liberal Arts, Texas A & M University, Public Policy Paper No. 10, 1984.

Battalio, R. C., Fisher, E. B., Kagel, J. H., Winkler, R. C., and Basmann, R. L., "A Test of Consumer Demand Theory Using Observations of Individual Consumer Purchases," *Western Economic Journal*, Vol. 11, 1973: 211-225.

Battalio, R. C., Kagel, J. H., Green, L., and Rachlin, H., "Consumer Demand Behavior with Pigeons as Subjects," *Journal of Political Economy*, Vol. 89, 1981a: 69-81.

Battalio, R. C. Green, L., and Kagel, J. H., "Income-Leisure Tradeoffs of Animal Workers," *American Economic Review*, Vol. 71, 1981b: 621-632.

Bergson, A., "Real Income, Expenditure Proportionality and Frisch's New Methods of Measuring Marginal Utility," *Review of Economic Studies*, Vol. 4, 1936: 32-52.

Berndt, E. R., Darrough, M. N., and Diewert, W. E., "Flexible Functional Forms and Expenditure Distributions: An Application to Canadian Consumer Demand Functions," *International Economic Review*, Vol. 18, 1977: 651-675.

Berndt, E. and E. Savin, "Estimation and Hypothesis Testing in Singular Equation Systems with Autoregressive Disturbances," *Econometrica*, Vol. 43, 1975: 937-957.

Blanciforti, L. "The Almost Ideal Demand System Incorporating Habits: An Analysis with Expenditures on Food and Aggregate Commodity Groups," Ph.D. Dissertation, University of California, Davis, 1982.

Blanciforti, L. and Green, R., "An Almost Ideal Demand System Incorporating Habits," *Review of Economics and Statistics*, Vol. 66, 1984: 511-515.

Caves, D. W. and Christensen, L. R., "Global Properties of Flexible Functional Forms," *American Economic Review*, Vol. 70 1980: 442-432.

Christensen, L. R., Jorgenson, D. W., and Lau, L. J., "Transcendental Logarithmic Utility Functions," *American Economic Review*, Vol. 65, 1975: 367-383.

Christensen, L. R., and Manser, M. E., "Cost of Living Indexes for U. S. Meat and Produce, 1947-1971," in *Household Production and Consumption*, ed. Nestor Terlecky, New York: National Bureau of Economic Research, 1975.

Clower, R. W., and Riley, J. G., "The Foundations of Money Illusion in a Neo-Classical Micro-Monetary Model: Comments," *American Economic Review*, Vol. 66, 1976: 184-185.

Cobb, C. W. and Douglas, Ph H., "A Theory of Production," *American Economic Review, Papers and Proceedings*, Vol. 18, 1928: 138-165.

Conrad, K., and Jorgenson, D. W., "Testing the Integrability of Demand Functions," *European Economic Review*, Vol. 12, 1979: 115-147.

de V. Graaff, J., *Theoretical Welfare Economics*, London: Cambridge University Press, 1967.

Deaton, A. and Muellbauer, J., *Economics and Consumer Behavior*, London: Cambridge University Press, 1980a.

Deaton, A. and Muellbauer, J., "An Almost Ideal Demand System," *American Economic Review*, Vol. 70, 1980b: 312-326.

Diamond, Charles A., "Nonparametric Cost-of-Living Indexes Rationalized by the Generalized Fechner-Thurstone Direct Utility Function and Changes in Labor and Demographic Patterns," Ph.D. Dissertation, Department of Economics, Texas A & M University, College Station, TX, 1984.

Diewert, W. E., "Applications of Duality Theory," in Frontiers of Quantitative Economics Vol II, ed. M.D. Intrilligator and D.A. Kendrick, Amsterdam: North Holland, 1974: 106-171.

Diewert, W. E., "Afriat and Revealed Preference Theory," *Review of Economic Studies*, Vol. 40, 1976: 419-425.

Diewert, W. E., "Exact and Superlative Index Numbers," *Journal of Econometrics*, Vol. 4, 1976: 115-145.

Diewert, W. C., "Superlative Index Numbers and Consistency in Aggregation," *Econometrica*, Vol. 46, 1978: 883-900.

Diewert, W. E., "The Economic Theory of Index Numbers," *Theory and Measurement of Consumer Behavior*, ed. Angus Deaton, Cambridge: Cambridge University Press, 1981.

Diewert, W. E. and Parkan, W., "Tests for the Consistency of Consumer Data and Nonparametric Index Numbers," Discussion Paper 78-27, Department of Economics, University of British Columbia, Vancouver, BC 1978.

Diewert, W. E. and Parkan, W., "Linear Programming Tests of Regularity Conditions for Production Functions," Discussion Paper 79-01, Department of Economics, University of British Columbia, Vancouver, BC 1979.

Duesenberry, J. S., Income, Savings, and the Theory of Consumer's Behavior, Cambridge, MA: Harvard University Press, 1949.

Durbin, J. and Watson, G. S., "Testing for Serial Correlation in Least Squares Regression, Part II," *Biometrica*, Vol. 37, 1950: 409-428.

Dusansky, R. and Kalman, R. J., "The Real Balance Effect and the Traditional Theory of Consumer Behavior: A Reconciliation," *Journal of Economic Theory*, Vol. 5, 1972: 336-346.

Dusansky, R. and Kalman, R. J., "Foundations of Money Illusion in a Neoclassical Micro-Monetary Model," *American Economic Review*, Vol. 64, 1974: 115-122.

Edwards. A. W. F., *Likelihood*, Cambridge: Cambridge University Press, 1972.

Econometric Society, "Report of the Kiel Meeting," *Econometrica*, Vol. 24, 1956: 299-337.

Fawson, Chris and Johnson, John D., "A Heuristic Approach to Reduce Model Development Complexity: An Application to Regional Agricultural Production," presented paper at the *Second International Conference on Economic Modelling*, University of London, London, England, March 28-30, 1988.

Fisher, F. M. and Shell, K., "Taste and Quality Change in the Pure Theory of the True Cost of Living Index," in *Value, Capital, and Growth: Papers in Honor of Sir John Hicks*, ed. J. N. Wolfe, Edinburgh: University of Edinburgh Press, 1968.

Fisher, Irving, *The Making of Index Numbers*, 3rd Edition, Boston: Houghton Mifflin Co. 1927.

Fisher, R. A., "On the Mathematical Foundations of Theoretical Statistics," *Phil. Trans.*, Royal Society London, Series A, Vol. 222, 1922: 390-368.

Fisher, R. A., *Statistical Methods and Scientific Inference*, New York: Hafner Publishing Company, 1956.

Franklin, Philip, *A Treatise on Advanced Calculus*, New York: John Wiley and Sons 1940.

Frentrup, John C., "An International Study of Nonparametric Cost- of-Living Indexes Derivable from the Generalized Fechner-Thurstone

Direct Utility Function," Ph.D. Dissertation, Department of Economics, Texas A & M University, College Station, TX, 1984.

Friedman, M., *Price Theory*, Chicago, IL: Aldine Publishing Company, 1962.

Gallant, R. A., "On the Bias in Flexible Functional Forms and an Essentially Unbiased Form: The Fourier Functional Form," *Journal of Econometrics*, Vol. 15, 1981: 221-245.

Geary, R. C., "A Note on the Constant Utility Index of the Cost of Living," *Review of Economic Studies*, Vol. 30, 1963: 65-66.

Gorman, W. M., "Additive Logarithmic Preferences: A Further Note," *Review of Economic Studies*, Vol. 30, 1963: 56-62.

Gorman, W. M., "Production Functions in Which the Elasticities of Substitution Stand in Fixed Proportion to Each Other," *Review of Economic Studies*, Vol. 32, 1965: 217-224.

Gorman, William, "Tastes, Habits and Choices," *International Economic Review*, Vol. 8, 1967: pp. 218-222.

Graybill, F., *Theory and Application of the Linear Model*, North Scituate: Duxbury Press, 1976.

Green, H. A., *Consumer Theory*, New York: Academic Press, 1978.

Hanoch, G., "CRESH Production Functions," *Econometrica*, Vol. 39, 1971: 695-712.

Hanoch, G., "Production and Demand Models with Direct or Indirect Implicit Additivity," *Econometrica*, Vol 43, 1975: 395-419.

Hansen, B., *A Survey of General Equilibrium Systems*, New York: McGraw-Hill, 1970.

Harberger, A. L., "Three Basic Postulates for Applied Welfare Economics," *Journal of Economic Literature*, Vol. 9, 1971: 785-797.

Hayakawa, H., "Consumer Theory When Prices and Real Income Affect Preferences," *Southern Economic Journal*, Vol. 43, 1976: 840-845.

Hayes, K.J., Molina, D.J. and Slottje, D.J., "Preference Variation Across North America," *Economica*, (forthcoming).

Hicks, J. R., *Value and Capital*, Oxford: Clarendon Press, 1946.

Hicks, J. R. and Allen, R. D. G., "A Reconsideration of the Theory of Value," *Economica*, N. S. 1, 1934: 52-75, 196-219.

Houthakker, H. S., "Revealed Preferences and the Utility Function," *Economica*, Vol. 17, 1950: 159-174.

Houthakker, H. S., "Additive Preferences," *Econometrica*, Vol. 28, 1960: 244-257.

Houthakker, H. S., "A Note on Self-Dual Preferences," *Econometrica*, Vol. 33, 1965: 797-801.

Houthakker, H. S. and Taylor, L.D., *Consumer Demand in the United States 1929-1970*, Cambridge, Mass.: Harvard University Press, 1970.

Ichimura, Shinichi, "A Critical Note on the Definition of Related Goods," *Review of Economic Studies*, Vol. 18, 1951: pp. 179-183.

James, W., *"Principles of Psychology*, Vol. I, New York: Dover Publications, 1890, Reprinted 1950.

Johnson, John D., "The Sensitivity of the Cost of Living to the Prices of Monetary Assets: A Variable Consumer Preference Approach," Ph.D. Dissertation, Department of Economics, Texas A & M University, College Station, Texas, Dec 1987.

Johnson, John D., "The Sensitivity of the Cost of Living to the Prices of Monetary Aggregates," Working Paper #, Department of Economics, Southern Methodist University, Dallas, TX 75275, 1988.

Johnson, H. G., "The Effects of Income Redistribution on Aggregate Consumption with Interdependence of Consumer Preferences," *Economica*, Vol. 19, 1952: 131-147.

Judge, G., Griffiths, W., Hill R.C., Lütkepohl, H., Lee, T., *The Theory and Practice of Econometrics*, second edition, New York: John Wiley and Sons, 1985.

Kagel, J. H., and R. Battalio, "Experimental Studies of Consumer Behavior using Laboratory Animals," *Economic Inquiry*, Vol. 13, 1981: 22-39.

Kalman, P. L., "Theory of Consumer Behavior When Prices Enter the Utility Function," *Econometrica*, Vol. 36, 1981: 497-510.

Kempe, F., "Quid Pro Quo: Poles Survive Collapse of Currency by Using Own System of Barter," *Wall Street Journal*, Oct. 23, 1981: 1, col. 1.

Kenkle, J., *Dynamic Linear Economic Models*, New York: Gordon and Breach Science Publishers, 1974.

King, M. C., "The Durbin-Watson Test for Serial Correlation: Bounds for Regressions with Trend and/or Seasonal Dummy Variables," *Econometrica*, Vol. 49, 1981: 1571-1583.

Klein, L. R. and Rubin, H. "A Constant Utility Index of the Cost of Living," *Review of Economic Studies*, Vol. 16, 1947-48: 84-87.

Kmenta, J., *Elements of Econometrics*, New York: Macmillan Press, 1971.

Koo, A. C., "An Empirical Test of Revealed Preference Theory," *Econometrica*, Vol. 31, 1963: 646-664.

Konyus, A. A., "The Problem of the True Index of the Cost of Living Index," Economic Bulletin of the Institute of Economic Conjecture, Moscow, 1924: No. 9-10. English translation *Econometrica*, Vol. 7, 1936: 110-129.

Koopmans, T. C., *Three Essays on the State of Economic Science*, New York: McGraw-Hill, Inc., 1957.

Kuhn, T. S., *The Structure of Scientific Revolutions*, Chicago: University of Chicago Press, 1962.

Lau, J., Lin W., and Totopoulous, P., "The Linear Logarithmic Expenditure System: An Application to Consumption-Leisure Choice," *Econometrica*, Vol. 46, 1978: 843-869.

Landsburg, Steven, "Taste Change in the United Kingdom: 1900- 1955," *Journal of Political Economy*, Vol. 89, #1, 1981: 92-104.

Layard, P. R. G. and Walters, A. A., *Microeconomic Theory*, McGraw-Hill, 1978.

Leibenstein, H., "Bandwagon, Snob and Veblen Effects in the Theory of Demand," *Quarterly Journal of Economics*, Vol. 64, 1950: 153- 207.

Leser, C. E. V., "Family Budget and Price-Elasticities of Demand," *Review of Economic Studies*, Vol. 9, 1941-42: 40-57.

Liebhafsky, H. H., "Preferences as a Function of Prices and Money Income," *Varta*, Vol. 1, 1980: 1-16.

Manser, M., "Elasticities of Demand for Food: An Analysis Using Non-additive Utility Functions Allowing for Habit Formation," *Southern Economic Journal*, Vol. 43, 1976: 879-891.

McKenzie, G. W., *Measuring Economic Welfare: New Methods*, Cambridge: Cambridge University Press, 1983.

Mood, A., Graybill, F. and Boes, D., *Introduction to the theory of Statistics*, Third Edition, New York: McGraw-Hill, 1974.

Mossin, A., "A Mean Demand Function and Individual Demand Functions Confronted with the Weak and Strong Axioms of Revealed Preferences: An Empirical Test," *Econometrica*, Vol. 40, 1972: 177-192.

Mukerji, V., "Generalized SMAC Function with Constant Ratios of Elasticities of Substitution," *Review of Economic Studies*, Vol. 30, 1963: 233-236.

Muellbauer, J., "Aggregation, Income Distribution, and Consumer Demand," *Review of Economic Studies*, Vol. 42, 1975 :525-543.

Ng, Y. K., *Welfare Economics*, New York: John Wiley and Sons, 1980.

Opiela, Tim, "An Empirical Investigation of Consistent Monetary Aggregates." Ph.D. Dissertation, Department of Economics, Texas A & M University, College Station, Texas, 1986.

Pandey, Ruby, "The Substitutability of Monetary Assets: A variable Preferences Approach," Ph.D. dissertation, Department of Economics, Texas A & M University, College Station, Texas, 1986.

Patinkin, D.,*Money, Interest and Prices*, New York: Harper and Row Publishing Company 1965.

Phlips, L., "A Dynamic Version of the Linear Expenditure Model " , *Review of Economics and Statistics*, Vol. 54, 1972: pp. 450-458.

Pollak, R. A., *The Theory of the Cost of Living Index*, Office of Prices and Living Conditions, U.S. Bureau of Labor Statistics, Research Discussion Paper No. 11, 1971.

Pollak, R. A., "Habit Formation and Long Run Utility Functions," Journal of Economic Theory, Vol. 13, 1976: pp. 272-297.

Pollak, R. A., "Price Dependent Preferences," *American Economic Review*, Vol. 67, 1977: pp. 64-75.

Pollak, R. A., "Endogenous Tastes in Demand and Welfare Analysis," *American Economic Review*, Vol. 68, 1978: 374-379.

Pollak, R.A. and Wales, T.J., "Estimation of the Linear Expenditure System," *Econometrica*, Vol. 37, 1969: 611-628.

Rosen, H., "The Measurement of Excess Burden with Explicit Utility Functions," *Journal of Political Economy*, Vol. 86, 1978: 5121-5137.

Roy, R., *De l'Utilite, Contribution a la Theorie des Choix*, Paris: Herman, 1943.

Samuelson, P. A., "A Note on the Pure theory of Consumer's Behavior," *Economica*, Vol. 5, 1938: 61-90.

Samuelson, P. A., "Some Implications of Linearity," *Review of Economic Studies*, Vol. 15, 1947a: 88-90.

Samuelson, P. A., *Foundations of Economic Analysis*, Cambridge: Harvard University Press, 1947b: 117.

Samuelson, P. A., "Consumption Theory in Terms of Revealed Preferences," *Economica*, 1948: 243-253.

Samuelson, P. A. and Swamy, S., "Invariant Economic Index Numbers and Canonical Duality: Survey and Synthesis," *American Economic Review*, Vol. 64, 1974: 566-593.

Samuelson, P. A. and Sato, R., "Unattainability of Integrability and Definiteness Conditions in the General Coarse of Demand for Money and Goods," *American Economic Review*, Vol. 74, 1984: 588-604.

Sato, K., "Additive Utility Functions with Double-Log Consumer Demand Functions," *Journal of Political Economy*, Vol. 80, 1972: 102-124.

Schultz, H., *The Theory and Measurement of Demand*, Chicago, IL: The University of Chicago Press, 1938.

Scitovsky, T., "Some Consequences of Judging Quality by Price," *Review of Economic Studies*, Vol. 11, 1944-45: 100-105.

Sen, A. K., *Collective Choice and Social Welfare*, San Francisco, CA: Holden Day & Edinburgh: Oliver and Boyd, 1970.

Sen, A. K., *On Economic Inequality*, Oxford: Clarendon Press, 1973.

Sen, A. K., "The Welfare Basis of Real Income Comparisons: A Survey," *Journal of Economic Literature*, Vol. 17, 1979: 1-45.

Seo, T. K., "A Generalization of Two Leading Systems of Demand Functions," Ph.D. Dissertation, Department of Economics Texas A & M University, College Station, Texas, 1973.

Shoven, J. B., and Whalley, J., "Applied General Equilibrium Models of Taxation and International Trade," *Journal of Economic Literature*, Vol. 12, 1984: 1007-1052.

Slutsky, E., "Sulia teoria del bilancio des consomatore," *Giornale deglio Economist*, Vol. 51, 1915: 1-26. English Trans. in *Readings in Price Theory* eds. Stigler and Boulding, Chicago: University of Chicago Press, 1952.

Smith, H., *The Russians*, New York: Ballantine Books, 1976.

Stecher, E. L., "An Empirical Estimation of the Parameters of the Joint Relative Frequency Function of Consumer Demand and Planned Income for the United States, 1952-1975," Ph.D. Dissertation, Department of Economics, Texas A & M University, College Station, TX, 1978.

Stigler, G. J. and Becker, G., "De Gustibus non est Disputandum," *American Economic Review*, Vol. 67, 1977: 76-90.

Stigler, G.J., "The Early History of Empirical Studies of Consumer Behavior", *Journal of Political Economy*, Vol. 62, 1954: pp. 95-113.

Stone, R., "Linear Expenditure Systems and Demand Analysis: An Application to the Pattern of British Demand," *The Economic Journal*, Vol. 64, 1954: 511-527.

Theil, H., "The Information Approach to Demand Analysis," *Econometrica*, Vol. 33, 1965: 67-87.

Theil, H., *Theory and Measurement of Consumer Demand*, Vol. A, Amsterdam: North-Holland, 1975.

Thursby, M., "The Resource Reallocation Costs of Fixed and Flexible Exchange Rates: A Multi-Country Extension," *Journal of International Economics*, Vol. 11, 1981: 487-493.

Thurstone, C. I., "The Indifference Function," *Journal of Social Psychology*, Vol. 2, 1931: 131-167.

Tintner, Gerhard, "External Economies in Consumption," in *Essays in Economics and Econometrics*, ed. Ralph W. Pfouts, Chapel Hill, NC: University of North Carolina Press, 1960: pp. 107-112.

Tintner, Gerhard, "Complementarity and Shifts in Demand," *Metroeconomica*, Vol. 4, 1952: 1-4.

Uspensky, J. V., *Introduction to Mathematical Probability*, New York: McGraw-Hill, 1937.

Veblen, Thorstein, *The Theory of the Leisure Class*, New York: MacMillan Company, 1899.

Veblen, Thorstein, "Professor Clark's Economics," *Quarterly Journal of Economics*, Vol. 22, 1908, reprinted in Veblen, T. (1969).

Veblen, Thorstein, "The Limitations of Marginal Utility," *Journal of Political Economy*, Vol. 17, 1909, reprinted in Veblen, T. (1969).

Veblen, Thorstein, *Marx, Race, Science and Economics*, New York: Capricorn Books, 1969.

Wichers, C. R., "The Foundations of Money Illusion in a Neoclassical Micro- Monetary Model: Comment," *American Economic Review*, Vol. 66, 1976: 186-191.

Wold, H., *Demand Analysis*, New York: John Wiley & Sons, Inc. 1953.

Zellner, A., "An Efficient Method of Estimating Seemingly Unrelated Regressions and Tests for Aggregation Bias," *Journal of the American Statistical Association*, Vol. 57, 1962: 348-368.

Zellner, A., D. S. Huang, and C. C. Chau, "Further Analysis of the Short-Run consumption Function with Emphasis on the Role of Liquid Assets," *Econometrica*, Vol. 33, 1965: 571-581.

Appendix A

The Five Commodity Groups

In her study, Blanciforti (1982) constructed eleven commodity group price
and expenditure indices, which are outlined in detail in Appendix B, from
data from the National Income and Product Accounts (NIPA) for the
Bureau of Economic Analysis. The eleven commodity groups included:

1. Food,

2. Alcohol and Tobacco,

3. Clothing,

4. Housing,

5. Utilities,

6. Transportation,

7. Medical Care,

8. Durable Goods,

9. Nondurable Goods,

10. Services, and

11. Miscellaneous Goods.

In this book, we have aggregated to five commodity groups by combining
the eleven groups as follows:

1. Food Group includes (1) and (2) above.

2. Clothing Group includes (3), (9) and (11) above.

3. Housing Group includes (4) and (5) above.

4. Durables Group includes (6) and (8) above.

5. Medical Care Group includes (7) and (10) above.

Appendix B

The Eleven Commodity Groups

Following is a Description of Expenditure Items Included in Each Aggregate Group: Eleven Commodities as outlined in Appendix A

Mnemonic	Explanation
(1) Food:	Food purchased for off-premise consumption excluding alcohol, purchased meals and beverages.
(2) Alcohol and Tobacco:	alcoholic beverages plus tobacco products.
(3) Clothing:	Shoes and other footwear, shoe cleaning and repairing, clothing and accessories except footwear; cleaning, laundering, dyeing, pressing, alteration, storage, and repair of garments; jewelry and watches, other.
(4) Housing:	Owner occupied non-farm dwellings, tenant occupied non- farm dwellings.

(5) Utilities: Electricity, gas, fuel oil and coal.

(6) Transportation: Tires, tubes, accessories and other parts; repair, greasing, washing, parking, storage, and rental; gasoline and oil; bridge, tunnel, ferry, and toll roads; insurance premiums less claims made, purchased local transportation, purchased intercity transportation.

(7) Medical Care: Drug preparation and sundries; physicians, dentists and other professional services; privately controlled hospitals and sanitariums; medical care, hospital, income loss and workmen's comp. insurance.

(8) Durable Goods: Furniture inc. mattresses and bedsprings; kitchen and other household appliances; china, glass and tableware, utensils, and other durable household furnishings; books and maps; wheel goods, durable toys, sports equipment, boats and pleasure aircraft; radio and T. V. receivers; new autos, net purchases of used autos, other motor vehicles.

(9) Other Non-Durables: Toilet articles and preparations; semidurable household furnishings; cleaning and polishing preparations, misc. household supplies and paper products; stationery and writing supplies; magazines, newspapers, and sheet music; nondurable toys and sport supplies; flowers, seeds, and potted plants.

(10) Other Services: Personal business expenditures; barbers, beauty shops, and baths; water and other sanitary services; telephone and telegraph; domestic services; other household operations; radio and T. V. repair; admissions to spectator amusements; clubs and fraternal organizations; parimutuel net receipts; other recreation; commercial participants amusements.

(11) Other Miscellaneous Private education and research; religious and welfare activities; net foreign travel; food furnished employees; food produced and consumed on farms; clothing furnished to military personnel; rental value of farm dwellings; other housing; ophthalmic products and orthopedic appliances